Ancestry of
Frederick Keith Heasman (1898-1960)
of Conneaut, Ohio

Compiled by Michael Conrad Swanson
2017

Ancestry of Frederick Keith Heasman (1898-1960) of Conneaut, Ohio

Cover photograph courtesy of Tom Lee

ISBN-13: 978-1973865056
ISBN-10: 197386505X

First Edition July 2017

Published by Storkarhu Media
Franklin, Tennessee, USA
www.storkarhu.com

Acknowledgments

I am grateful for the help I received in compiling this book. Rebecca Swanson, Petra Marandi Roos, Steph Swanson, and Mark Swanson provided comments on the introduction. Kate Crosby of Hartfield, England, sent me pictures of Hindleap Lodge. Fran Box of the Steep History Group sent me church records from All Saints' Church in Steep, England. I wish to thank Jeff Lebzelter of Conneaut, Ohio, for unearthing newspaper articles and pictures about the Heasmans in Conneaut and Cindy Burns Eigel for sharing photos in Jeff's "People in Conneaut History" Facebook group. I am grateful to the numerous contributors to The Weald website (theweald.org). I thank Tom Lee for his permission to use his photograph of Ashdown Forest for the cover.

Michael Conrad Swanson
Franklin, Tennessee
July 2017

Organization

This book is divided into several chapters including an introduction, four descendant reports, a multi-page ancestor chart, an ancestor report, a photo gallery, and a name index. Each report and chart explores Frederick Keith "Keith" Heasman's family tree from a different perspective.

The introduction traces the Kerr (Keith's mother's maiden name) and Heasman lines back to Ulster, a province in the north of Ireland, and to Sussex, an historic county in southeastern England.

The four descendant reports start with Keith's great-grandparents -- the Heasmans, Stubbs, Kerrs, and Allinghams -- and follow their descendants down to Keith. The first person mentioned in the reports has the number 1, and subsequent people mentioned are assigned sequential numbers. A plus sign indicates the person appears later in the report.

The ancestor chart and ancestor report start with Keith and progress through several generations into the past. The earliest ancestors in the chart and report are his ninth great-grandparents John Heasman and William Gatland of Sussex County, England.

The ancestor report can be hard to navigate for those unfamiliar with the "ahnentafel" numbering system. The first person in the report, Keith, has the ahnentafel number 1, his father has the number 2, and his mother has the number 3. Numbers are assigned to ancestors according to a simple rule: a child's number is X, the father's number is 2 times X, the mother's number is 2 times X plus 1. Thus, if a person's number is 10 then the father's number is 20 and the mother's number is 21. The aforementioned William Gatland has an ahnentafel number of 2378, which means his daughter Annis Gatland's ahnentafel number is half that, or 1189.

The picture gallery includes photos and drawings of the Kerr's and Heasman's home towns and local landmarks in Ireland, England, Canada, and Ohio, as well as photos of the Kerrs, Heasmans, and their families.

Table of Contents

Table of Contents

Introduction

This book presents the ancestry of Frederick Keith "Keith" Heasman (1898-1960) of Conneaut, Ohio. Keith was a first-generation American born in 1898 in West Springfield, Pennsylvania. His parents were Frederick Huston "F.H." Heasman (1869-1952), born in England, and Elinor "Nellie" Kerr (1870-1918), born in Canada. The Heasmans have their roots near Ashdown Forest in the south of England and the Kerrs were from Ulster Province in the north of Ireland. Keith married Marion Katherine Rogers (1898-1992) of Conneaut in 1919 where they had one child, Patricia Ann. Keith and his brother, Darrell Esmond "Red" Heasman (1901-1954), ran Heasman's Grocery in Conneaut.

This book provides glimpses into the lives of Keith's ancestors through parish records, censuses, city directories, wills, and land records. An attempt was made to trace Keith's ancestry as far back as possible on all paternal and maternal branches, and several were traced to the 1500s. Among his ancestors were those who lived during the reign of Bloody Mary, maintained a royal hunting park, witnessed street-fighting in England's Second Civil War, became religious nonconformists, rubbed shoulders with Charles Darwin, survived the Irish Potato Famine, helped build an historic British railway, endured a six-week Atlantic voyage on a sailing ship, and became successful main street merchants and entrepreneurs. The birthplaces and addresses of Keith's immigrant ancestors in England and Ireland were discovered, so today it's possible to walk in their footsteps and have a pint in their pubs.

The Kerr Line

In Scotland, members of Clan Kerr lived in the Scottish Borders region adjacent to England. Clan Kerr soldiers, it is said, were trained to hold their swords with their left hands because it disconcerted the enemy. The term "kerr-handed" means left-handed in Scotland. The clan motto is *Sero Sed Serio* (Late But in Earnest). They "earned" their motto at the Battle of Ancrum Moor in 1545, in which they were mercenaries fighting with the English but changed sides and fought with their fellow Scots near the end of the battle.

The Kerrs -- those in Elinor Kerr's line -- were part of the Ulster Plantation, a "land grab" by King James I who created an English Protestant colony in the north of Ireland. The Ulster Plantation began in 1609 after the Irish chiefs of Ulster province fled in 1607 to France anticipating an English invasion. Their land was seized and given to English and Scottish settlers.

The Hume estate was established in 1610 as part of the Ulster Plantation by Scottish nobleman Sir John Hume who was given 2000 acres in County Fermanagh, Ireland. He built Tully Castle in 1619 on the southern shore of a 26-mile-long lake called the Lower Lough Erne. The castle was sacked in 1641 by an Irishman trying to take back his family's land.

The Kerrs settled on the Hume estate in the townland of Mullaghanelly, also known as Carrick. Many Irish church and census records were destroyed in a fire in Dublin in 1922, but other records suggest the Kerrs were in Carrick by the late 1600s. In 1672, Andrew Kerr was a churchwarden in Drumenagh Church near Carrick. George Kerr was churchwarden there in 1736 and another George Kerr succeeded him in 1790. In 1742, George Kerr of Carrick was listed on the Hume estate tax roll. In 1751, George Kerr and Gabriel Kerr were listed as freeholders (landowners) in Carrick. This George Kerr is probably Keith's fourth great-grandfather.

The word Carrick is an Anglicized version of the Gaelic word "carraig" (rock). Carrick contained only four or five homes on 129 acres of rolling pasture. Nearby, on Carrick Lake, are the ruins of Carrick Church (*Teampall Carraig*) built in the 1400s. The townland of Carrick lies a mile west of Tully Castle, a mile north of Derrygonnelly, and just south of Lough Navar Forest. The high hills of Lough Navar Forest provide panoramic views over much of the Fermanagh countryside and Lower Lough Erne.

Introduction

2x Great-Grandfather of Keith Heasman: George Kerr Sr. (c1780-)

Although documents show that the Kerrs were in Carrick in the 1600s, Elinor Kerr's proven paternal line starts with Keith Heasman's second great-grandfather, George Kerr Sr. (c1780-). George Kerr Sr. and Margaret Eaton of Carrick had five children in Carrick: Elizabeth, John, Jane (died in infancy), Jane, and George Jr. George Jr. was Keith's great-grandfather.

Great-Grandfather of Keith Heasman: George Kerr Jr. (1814-)

Sometime before 1862, George Kerr Jr. (1814-) moved a mile south from Carrick to Derrygonnelly, Ireland, where he leased a home with a garden on Main Street and a farm plot just north in Sandhill townland.

Derrygonnelly was a small hamlet in the mid-1700s until it established monthly market fairs in 1800. In 1812 they built a road along the Sillies River that became the village's main street with pubs, stores, and homes. To the west of Derrygonnelly are the picturesque limestone cliffs of Knockmore and to the east is the Lower Lough Erne.

George and his wife Jane had two sons, Thomas and Andrew. Andrew was Keith's grandfather. The Potato Famine (1845-1850) struck Ireland when Andrew was seven and caused dire poverty and mass starvation. The area including Derrygonnelly and Carrick lost a third of its population to death and emigration.

The economic depression after the famine lingered for years. A decade after the famine, George Jr.'s sons immigrated to Ontario, Canada -- Thomas in 1860 and Andrew in 1862.

Thomas Kerr (1837-1904) and his wife Margaret Craig (1841-1919) raised their family in Hamilton Township, Northumberland County, Ontario. Two of their sons were Canadian soldiers in World War I and both died before the end of the war. One son, Private George Kerr, was killed in action in November 1916 at Courcelette, France, and is memorialized at the Canadian National Vimy Memorial in Pas de Calais, France. Another son, Private Thomas Kerr, died of carbolic poisoning in May 1916 before his unit was shipped overseas in October 1916.

Grandfather of Keith Heasman: Andrew Kerr (c1838-1910)

Andrew Kerr (c1838-1910) married Jane Allingham in 1859 at Saint Ninnidh's Anglican Church near Derrygonnelly. They had one child in Ireland, Margaret Jane "Jennie." On March 20, 1862 they left Ireland from Londonderry on the three-masted steamship *Jura* for an eleven-day journey to Quebec.

Andrew was a farmer in Hamilton Township, Ontario. The children born to Andrew and Jane in Ontario were Mary, William, Elinor "Nellie," and Charlotte Elizabeth "Lottie." Elinor was Keith's mother. Andrew's first wife, Jane, died in 1884 in Hamilton and later the same year he married Ann Coomb. Andrew died in 1910 in Cobourg, Ontario.

Cobourg is a port town on the shore of Lake Ontario and Hamilton Township is a rural township surrounding Cobourg on three sides. By the 1830s, Cobourg's busy harbor made it a regional trade center. The largest business in Cobourg, and one of the largest operations of its kind in Canada, was the Ontario Woollen Mills, which opened in early 1846 and employed 170 people. The Woollen Mills was four and a half stories tall and manufactured over 400,000 yards of cloth a year. The Cobourg town hall, called Victoria Hall, is an extravagant, neoclassical three-story civic center built in 1848 during a period of prosperity. When the Kerrs arrived in the 1860s, Cobourg was suffering an economic depression, but by the early 1900s Cobourg was a revitalized summer vacation spot where tourists enjoyed the beach, sailing regattas, and yachting.

Introduction

Mother of Keith Heasman: Elinor Kerr (1870-1918)

Elinor "Nellie" Kerr (1870-1918) was raised in Hamilton Township, Ontario. In 1891, at the age of 21, Nellie was living with her sisters Jennie and Lottie in a Cobourg boarding house owned by Elizabeth Bond. Nellie and Jennie were dress makers.

Nellie's sister, Mary Ann, married George McCullough in Cobourg. Her brother, William, married Rose Maud "Birdie" Gibbs in Ontario and settled in Cobourg. Nellie and Jennie moved to Erie County, Pennsylvania, where they were married one day apart. Jennie married Joseph Talling, a car mechanic, on August 6, 1894 in Corry, Erie County, Pennsylvania. Emily married F.H. Heasman on August 7 in Corry.

Nellie and F.H. raised their children, Frederick Keith "Keith" and Darrell Esmond "Red," in Conneaut, Ohio. Nellie passed away in Conneaut in 1918 at the age of 48.

The Heasman Line

Shortly after William the Conqueror invaded and occupied England in 1066, a royal hunting park was created 30 miles south of London in an area of southeast England known as the Weald. The 20-square-mile park, called Ashdown Forest (also known as Lancaster Great Park from the 1300s to the 1600s), was surrounded by manors owned by noble families who, alongside princes and kings, used the park for grand deer and boar hunts. Commoners used the park to graze livestock and cut bracken (ferns) for animal bedding. Game poachers and squatters risked arrest by the Crown's forest keepers.

The Heasmans were commoners who lived near Ashdown Forest for hundreds of years. The Heasman surname, which is derived from the Old English words "haess" (brushland) and "mann" (man), suggests an ancient connection to the park.

The Heasmans moved among several Sussex County villages and towns around Ashdown Forest. On the west side of Ashdown Forest they lived in the villages of Barcombe and West Hoalthy. On the north side they resided in East Grinstead, Coleman's Hatch, and Hartfield. On the east side they lived in Withyham and Rotherfield. On the south side they resided in Little Horsted and Buxted.

Most of these towns were listed in the 1086 "Great Survey" of England and Wales which was nicknamed the Domesday Book. The word Domesday is derived from the Old English words "domes" (dooms) and "daeg" (day). Commissioned by William the Conqueror, the survey was so comprehensive that it reminded some of the biblical Book of Life of the Last Judgement, or Doomsday, which listed every redeemed soul.

Well-known historical sites near Ashdown Forest include Bolebroke Castle, Hever Castle, and Buckhurst Park. Bolebroke was Henry VIII's hunting lodge; Hever was the childhood home of Henry VIII's second wife, Queen Anne Boleyn; and Buckhurst, home of the noble family Sackwell, was the setting for the "Hundred Acre Wood" in A. A. Milne's books *Winnie-the-Pooh* (1926) and *The House at Pooh Corner* (1928).

9x Great-Grandfather of Keith Heasman: John Heasman (-1558)

John Heasman (-1558), Keith's ninth great-grandfather, is the earliest ancestor found in Keith's paternal line. John lived most of his life during the reign of Henry VIII (1491-1547, reign 1509-1547) and his last few years during the reign of Queen "Bloody" Mary (1516-1558, reign 1553-1558). During her brief reign she ordered hundreds of Brits and dozens of Sussex County residents burned at the stake for resisting conversion to Catholicism.

John Heasman was a husbandman (tenant farmer) in Barcombe, Sussex, a rural village southwest of Ashdown Forest. The name Barcombe is derived from the Old English words "bere" (barley) and "camp" (open space), a reference to the area's barley fields. John leased

Introduction

farmland and buildings on two tracts called "Sewells farm" and "Lakers" in the ancient manor of Rodmell. He and his wife Alice (surname unknown) had a daughter, Jone (an old spelling of Joan), and two sons, John and William. William was Keith's eighth great-grandfather.

8x Great-Grandfather of Keith Heasman: William Heasman (1551-1616)

William Heasman (1551-1616) was a freeholder (landowner) in Barcombe and a resident of nearby Little Horsted. His more than 60 acres in Rodmell manor included the tracts called "Lakers" and "Newlands." A farm of this size would have constituted a good estate at the time. William surpassed his father in social rank, becoming a yeoman, which meant he owned his land outright. He was called a gentleman in 1614 court documents, briefly stepping up onto the lowest rung of English gentry, although in his will he refers to himself as a yeoman.

William Heasman probably married twice, first to Elizabeth Cayley and last to Ann (surname unknown) who is mentioned in his will. William's children were Mary, Anne, Francis, and Susan. Francis was Keith's seventh great-grandfather.

7x Great-Grandfather of Keith Heasman: Francis Heasman (1590-1667)

Francis Heasman (1590-1667) benefitted from his father's rising social status. In 1610, Francis was a gentleman, a social rank that made him eligible for a variety of positions of civic responsibility. Francis was appointed the keeper of Hindleap and deputy to Richard Sackville, Earl of Dorset and Master of Ashdown Forest. Hindleap was the northwest section of Ashdown Forest.

Ashdown Forest was managed by six keepers who were stationed around the perimeter of the park. Each keeper was given a dwelling, a couple dozen acres, and a barn or two. A keeper's duties included maintaining the park gates and the fence-and-ditch system (called the pale) surrounding the park; arresting poachers, squatters and clay diggers; and breeding deer and boar. In short, they kept the park ready for the royal hunts.

Francis married Bridget Foord of Buxted, Sussex. Their first two children, Francis and Thomas, were baptized at Saint Margaret the Queen Church in Buxted. The church was built in 1250 and the original structure remains largely intact. In 1543, the first English cast iron cannons were made in Buxted.

Their other children -- John (died in infancy), John, Rose, Elizabeth, Anthony -- were baptized four miles north of Hindleap at Saint Swithun's Church in East Grinstead. Their son John was Keith's sixth great-grandfather.

Francis's father, William, died in 1616 and willed his farmland to Francis, which would have required him to return to Barcombe to manage the farm and pay land taxes. Francis chose, however, to continue as keeper at Hindleap and so he forfeited his inheritance.

In 1646, Francis received a letters patent (a legal document issued by the Crown) which re-appointed him to his position at Hindleap and made him the deputy of Philip Herbert, Fourth Earl of Pembroke and Master of Game in Ashdown. Francis was the keeper at Hindleap at least through 1658 when his home was surveyed for Parliament by William Webb:

"Hindleap Lodge: All that messuage dwelling house or lodge scittuate and Lodge being in the fforest or chace aforesaid in the present occupacon of Ffrancis Hesman in the parish of East Greensteed commonly called or knowne by the name of Hind Leap lodge consisting of a Hall, Parlor Kitchin, and other necessary Roomes below Staires wth three chambers besides Garretts above staires, wth a barne, stable, gardine and severall parcells of land formerly inclosed adjoyning belonging and commonly used wth the said Messuage dwelling house or lodge conteyning by admeasurement twenty foure acres vallue p ann 24acr."

Introduction

By the time King Charles I was executed in 1649, the royal hunts at Ashdown had come to an end. Francis would live to see the monarchy restored in 1660, but within a few decades half the forest was divided among noblemen, the pale around the forest had fallen into disrepair, and the wild deer were gone.

Francis died in 1667 and Bridget died in 1669. They were buried at Saint Margaret's Church in West Hoathly.

In 1693, part of Hindleap was converted into a rabbit farm called Hindleap Warren. About 200 years later, Hindleap would serve a new purpose: in 1898, James Bryce, Ambassador to the United States, built a large cottage at Hindleap and used the keeper's lodge as his office. Today, Hindleap Warren is an educational nature park for youth and the restored keeper's lodge is a private residence.

6x Great-Grandfather of Keith Heasman: John Heasman (1621-1698)

John Heasman (1621-1698) married Susan Heritage (c1620-c1651) in 1644 in East Grinstead. After Susan died, he married Ann Bane (1634-) in 1658, also in East Grinstead. Ann Bane's parents were Cornelius Bane, a stone mason in East Grinstead, and An Cormucke. John Heasman had a total of eleven children. With Susan he had Henry, Katherine, and Susannah. With Ann he had William, Elizabeth (died in infancy), Elizabeth (died young), Richard, Edward, John, Robert, and Elizabeth. All the children were baptized at Saint Swithun's Church. Edward was Keith's fifth great-grandfather.

Notice that three of their children were named Elizabeth. The practice of re-using children's names was common because of the high infant mortality rate. Re-used names were used to honor deceased younger siblings and to preserve the name of a parent or grandparent for the next generation.

John Heasman and the next three generations in the line lived near Ashdown Forest in East Grinstead Parish. The name East Grinstead -- Estgrensted in the Domesday Book -- comes from the Old English words "grenen" (green) and "stede" (place). East Grinstead is a market town with one of the longest continuous runs of fourth-century timber-framed buildings in England. Saint Swithun's Church (sometimes spelled Swithin) in East Grinstead was built in 1078 and rebuilt twice after it collapsed, first in the 1300s and the current building in the 1780s.

5x Great-Grandfather of Keith Heasman: Edward Heasman (1666-1737)

John's son Edward Heasman (1666-1737) married Jane (surname unknown) about 1688 and had five children -- William, John Robert, Elizabeth, and Edward -- who were all baptized at Saint Swithun's Church in East Grinstead. William was Keith's fourth great-grandfather.

4x Great-Grandfather of Keith Heasman: William Heasman (1689-1772)

William Heasman (1689-1772) married Rachel Medhurst (1702-1775) at Saint Thomas a Becket Church in Framfield, Sussex. Their children -- William, John, Robert, Edward, Thomas, James, Henry, Samuel, Elizabeth (died young), and Elizabeth -- were all baptized at Saint Swithun's Church. Samuel was Keith's third great-grandfather.

Rachel Medhurst's parents were William Medhurst, a pail maker, and Elizabeth Cornwell of Framfield. Elizabeth Cornwell descended from craftsmen in Framfield who worked as carpenters, spoon makers, and pail makers.

Rachel Medhurst's great-grandparents, John Medhurst (c1615-) and Repentance West of Maidstone in Kent County, were witnesses to the 1648 Battle of Maidstone during the Second Civil War. The Parliament had grown more religiously conservative and declared that religious holidays were vulgar and unbiblical. The war began in December 1647 when the town crier in

Introduction

Canterbury, Kent, proclaimed that Christmas Day would become a regular workday. In defiance of the order, town folk decorated doorways with holly and kept their shops closed -- and later rioted. On June 1, about 4000 parliamentary troops stormed Maidstone to quell continuing civil disturbances and protests. Parliamentary troops fought street by street and defeated the royalist troops, resulting in about 1000 casualties. Thirteen years later, in 1660, the monarchy was restored and King Charles II nullified the anti-Christmas law.

3x Great-Grandfather of Keith Heasman: Samuel Heasman (1736-1815)

Samuel Heasman (1736-1815) married Sarah Wheatley (1740-1806) of West Hoathly at Saint Swithun's in 1760. Sarah was the daughter of Edward Wheatley, a weaver in East Grinstead, and Ann Vinall. William and Sarah had eight children: John, Samuel, Sarah, Edward, Anna, William, James, and Susanna. James was Keith's second great-grandfather.

2x Great-Grandfather of Keith Heasman: James Heasman (1775-1859)

James Heasman (1775-1859) married Elizabeth Turk (1779-1845) at Saint Swithun's Church in 1797. Elizabeth was the daughter of Thomas Turk, a farmer, and his wife Mary.

James was an agricultural laborer, which meant he was hired to work on others' farms. James and Elizabeth had eight children: Samuel, Thomas, Sarah, Susanna, Henry, Solomon, Mary, and Lucy. Samuel was Keith's great-grandfather.

Their first two children were baptized at Saint Swithun's Church. However, starting with Sarah, their children were no longer baptized in the Anglican state church. Their births were recorded, instead, in the Nonconformist Register. There is no indication of why they left the church, but Quaker, Baptist, and Wesleyan Methodist meeting houses were nearby.

As an historical aside, Elizabeth Turk's grandfather, John Turk (1712-1787), had some difficulty marrying his fiancé and first cousin, Sarah Brown (1717-1793). Unable to secure a marriage license in their parish, they traveled to London in 1740 for a "clandestine" marriage. Couples who could not obtain a marriage license went to the courtyard outside Fleet Prison to receive a street-side, no-questions-asked marriage. (They were not the only couple in the family to be married at Fleet Prison. John Heasman, the son of Keith's fourth great-grandparents, William Heasman and Rachel Medhurst, also had a Fleet wedding, but in his case he was 16 -- underage -- and his bride was 22.)

James and Elizabeth's family first lived in a cottage in Ashdown Forest at Wych Cross (a reference to Saint Richard de Wych), adjacent to Hindleap. They moved to a cottage at nearby Quabrook Common in Coleman's Hatch, a hamlet halfway between East Grinstead and Hartfield.

The name Coleman's Hatch -- spelled Colemanhacche in the 1400s -- refers to the "hacche" (gate) into Ashdown Forest and to the Coleman family who lived there in the 1300s. In 1496, at Newbridge Pond near Coleman's Hatch, French ironmasters built Britain's first water-powered blast furnace. In the 1700s, a row of cottages built in 1430 were converted into Coleman's Hatch Public House, which is still a bustling pub and restaurant today. The current owners say the pub was once owned by a Heasman. In the mid-1800s, the preeminent biologist Charles Darwin (1809-1882) often visited his sister-in-law at her home called South Hartfield House in Coleman's Hatch. Darwin took walks in Ashdown Forest where he studied carnivorous plants. The opening words of his book *Insectivorous Plants* (1875) are: "During the summer of 1860, I was surprised by finding how large a number of insects were caught by the leaves of the common sundew (Drosera rotundifolia) on a heath in Sussex. I had heard that insects were thus caught, but knew nothing further on the subject."

Introduction

Great-grandfather of Keith Heasman: Samuel Heasman (1799-1855)

James's son Samuel Heasman (1799-1855) married Sarah Shoebridge (1806-1872) at Saint Swithun's Church in 1824. Sarah was the daughter of Jesse Shoebridge, a farmer, and Karen Weller. Samuel was an agricultural laborer. The family lived in a cottage in Graddock's Pit Wood (also called Cabbagestalk) in West Hartfield.

Samuel and Sarah had eight children, all of whom were baptized at Saint Mary's Church in Hartfield: Harriett, Philadelphia, Jane, Jesse, Mary, Thomas, Ann, Hannah, and Emily. Thomas was Keith's grandfather. When Samuel died, Sarah moved with the children from Graddock's Pit to a cottage at Marsh Green in Coleman's Hatch.

In 1841, Sarah Shoebridge's parents, Jessie Shoebridge and Karen Weller, lived in a timber framed cottage called Lower Pest House Number 2 in Hartfield. Lower Pest House still stands and is a protected historic building called Larkspur. The three parish "pest houses" (pestilence houses) in Hartfield were used to quarantine people with communicable diseases such as smallpox and the plague. These pest houses were converted to regular cottages about the 1830s, but they kept their gloomy names.

Hartfield -- spelled Hertevel in the Domesday Book -- is derived from the Old English words "heorot" (stag) and "feld" (pasture), a reference to wild deer. Hartfield's Saint Mary's Church was built in the 1200s and its tower was built in the 1300s. Landmarks in Hartfield are Bolebroke Castle, Cotchford Farm (the home of A.A. Milne), Buckhurst Park (the setting for Milne's "Hundred Acre Wood"), and the Hammerwood estate. Hammerwood manor was built in 1792 by Henry Latrobe (1764-1820), the architect for the White House and U.S. Capitol Building. The manor was purchased in the 1970s by the band Led Zeppelin and completely restored in the 1980s by new owners.

The Heasmans were commoners whose use of the forest was sometimes opposed by local nobility. However, the ancient "rights of common," supported by the Crown, allowed commoners to use ten square miles of Ashdown Forest to graze animals, collect wind-blown branches and trees, and cut litter (heather and ferns) for animal bedding. These rights were challenged by local nobility in a famous legal dispute called the Great Ashdown Forest Case (1876-1882). Samuel Heasman's brother, Henry Heasman (1806-1893), was interviewed for the trial because the court wanted some history about how commoners used the forest. The commoners initially lost the case, but on appeal they won a limited right to cut and take litter from the forest. The victory lead to expanded land-use laws enacted over the next century. Here is Henry's testimony, which gives a glimpse into the life of commoners living near Ashdown Forest:

"Heasman, Henry. Living at the house called the Chequers in Forest Row. Retired laborer. I was born 14 July 1805 at Little Parrock Farm. I was not baptised till I was grown up. My maternal grandfather named Turk used the Farm and my Father worked for him. When I first recollect anything I was living half way between Little Parrock and Forest Row. When I was about 8 years old, my Father moved to a cottage in the Forest close by Quabrook Common. The house is pulled down now and the land is used by Dick Card. My Father and Mother died there and I continued to live there with my grandfather till I married.

"The first job I ever did was to rake up the litter my Father cut on the Forest. That was before I left going to school when I was about 10. I worked with my Father till I was about 15. He used to work as a sawyer in the summer and also cut turf and peat on the Forest and in the winters he used to go out on the Forest litter cutting. I went to live with Mr. Holland at Fairlee Farm on the Michaelmas after I was 15. This farm is near East Grinstead town and belongs to the Cranstone Trustees. I remained there a year working as carter boy and going with the ox team. I then went to Little Oasted Farm close by, used by Mr. Shoebridge and lived with him a year as a carter boy. Then to Kennards at the White Horse at Holtye Common and worked on the farm as carter boy for the winter 1/2 year. Then I went home and worked with my Father till I married, sawing and

Introduction

cutting turf in summer and cutting wood and litter in the winter. I married when I was 24 or 25. A few months after I went to live at a cottage at Quabrook Common belonging to old Master Heaver who had Tablehurst Farm and Mill.

"For 11 years I worked about in the summer and cut litter in the winter. I then moved to Pigstyes Farm house close to the station used by Mr. Turner and lived there about 17 years working at sawing and litter cutting. I then moved to a cottage by the school on Forest Row Green for about a year. I then lived in an old house in Forest Row under Mr. Isted 11 or 12 years and worked for Kidbrook Park about 12 years. Then I moved to the Chequers at Forest Row for about 3 years and have lived there ever since.

"Before I went to service when I worked with my Father he used to cut litter for the Hon. Anne Fuller at Ashdown House which used to be called Lavertye. He cut a great deal for her, also for Mr. Jeffery who then owned the farm now belonging to Colonel Moor what was and still is called Pixtons and for old miller Heaver who used Tablehurst. He used to have a great deal of litter. Also for General Ivory who lived at Thornhill and used a good deal of land by Ashurst Wood. Great Surrys belonged to it. He used to send 2 teams after it. Also for Godly at Upper Parrock and Fry, who then used Lines Farm and Ricelands. Also for Colonel Young who used Holly Hill and Snow's Hole and afterwards for Captain Hall and for Major Falconer who used Forest House. Also for old butcher Isted at Forest Row who used Pigstyes Farm. Also for Mr. Burt who had Stonehouse. Also for old Mr. Payne who lived at Leggs Heath. I used to see Parkhurst cutting. He lived at Furnace Farm now belonging to Mr. Melville. Also old Foster who lived at Clay Pits, belonging now to Mr. Hale, I saw his sons cutting after him. Hills at that time had Coleman's Hatch Public House and I used to see his boys out cutting brakes for his pigs."

The ten-square-mile commons of Ashdown Forest was almost lost in the 1980s when the owner, William Herbrand Sackville, 10th Earl De La Warr, offered it for sale. British Petroleum was interested in the land for oil wells, but conservationists -- including Christopher Robin Milne -- raised enough money to help the county buy and preserve it.

Grandfather of Keith Heasman: Thomas Heasman (1839-1916)

Samuel's son, Thomas Heasman (1839-1916), left Sussex County to seek a better life than subsistence farming and day labor could provide. Thomas was born at Graddock's Pit and was an agricultural laborer. About 1860, he moved 50 miles west to Ropley village near the town of New Alresford (or simply Alresford, pronounced Als-ford) in Hampshire County (abbreviated Hants).

Ropley, about 20 miles north of Portsmouth, was mentioned in the Domesday Book for providing the honey used to make William the Conqueror's mead. However, the area is best known for watercress. Watercress was harvested from New Alresford's chalk rivers and streams for centuries, but it was too perishable for transport by horse and cart to distant markets.

In New Alresford, Thomas found work with the Mid-Hants Railway Company which was building a railway to London. The new railway, completed in 1865, allowed watercress farmers in Hants to ship fresh watercress overnight to Covent Garden, London. Hants soon became England's main watercress producer. Today, the popular Alresford Watercress Festival annually celebrates the crop's value to the community. The Alresford Station and a portion of the railway is protected and operated as a heritage railway called the Watercress Line.

In 1865, Thomas married Emily Stubbs (1842-1928) in Ropley, England. Their first three children -- Frank, Frederick Huston "F.H.," and Fannie -- were born in New Alresford. Frederick Huston was Keith's father.

In the early 1870s, the government of Ontario, Canada, distributed flyers to workers in England which encouraged immigration. In 1873, Thomas Heasman and his family boarded a sailing vessel bound for Quebec. The trip took six weeks and upon arrival they moved to Cobourg, Ontario. In Cobourg they joined the Bible Christian (Wesleyan Methodist) Church and had three more

Introduction

children: William, Alberta, and Ernest.

In Canada, Thomas Heasman was employed by the Grand Trunk Railway. The original Grand Trunk line connected Montreal to Toronto. In 1873, the Grand Trunk Railway Company extended the line and began converting existing track to the standard gauge. Thomas Heasman worked for the railroad for a time, then took up farming and later became a milk dealer in Cobourg.

Father of Keith Heasman: Frederick Huston Heasman (1869-1952)

Frederick Huston "F.H." Heasman (1869-1952) immigrated as a child with his family to Canada in 1873. F.H. started working at age 11, first for a grocer and later on a tugboat. At 21, he was working as a wool weaver in Cobourg with his siblings at the Ontario Woollen Mills.

Before F.H. married Elinor "Nellie" Kerr (1842-1928) in 1894, he listed his residence as Harris, Ontario. They married in Corry, Erie County, Pennsylvania, and shortly afterwards he worked as a grocer in West Springfield, Erie County. There they had their first child, Frederick Keith, in 1898. Their second son, Darrell Esmond, was born in Conneaut, Ashtabula County, Ohio in 1901. A year after Nellie died in 1918, F.H. married Gertrude Zundel (1885-1972) in Conneaut.

West Springfield and Conneaut are neighboring towns on the shore of Lake Erie. The names Erie and Conneaut are derived from words in the Iroquoian language and the name Ashtabula is derived from an Algonquin word meaning "river of many fish."

When F.H. arrived in 1894, Erie County was an important shipbuilding and railroad hub while Conneaut was a growing, prosperous town with a ship port, a railroad hub, a rubber factory, a chair factory, a tool factory, a canning plant, a shovel factory, and a busy main street. In 1892, the first iron ore was received in Conneaut Harbor. In 1896, Andrew Carnegie expanded rail service at the port. In 1899 and 1900, several steam-powered "Hulett" unloaders went into service in Conneaut Harbor. In 1899, train car coal dumpers were installed that could load 25 tons of coal an hour. Soon, Conneaut Harbor was busy unloading ore bound for Pittsburgh and loading coal bound for port cities on the Great Lakes.

About 1898, F.H. opened Fred H. Heasman's General Store at 427 State Street and soon after F.H. Heasman Shoes on 412 Broad Street. About 1905, he formed a partnership with two other Conneaut businessmen called the Union Mercantile Company. In 1911, F.H. bought a grand, multi-story building on the northeast corner of Main and Mill Streets -- formerly called the Baldwin Block -- where he opened a dry goods store and a grocery store.

F.H.'s brother Frank Heasman, a loom tuner (loom mechanic) in Cobourg, had a parallel retail career in Canada. Frank opened Heasman's General Store in Barrie, Ontario, where he later bought the "old Imperial Bank block" to expand the operation. His brother, William Heasman, a wool spinner in Cobourg and a clerk in Conneaut, moved to Moose Jaw, Saskatchewan, where he opened a millinery (a hat store) in 1916. The store operated as Heasman's Furs and Fashions from the 1940s and closed in 2004. His brother, Sgt. Ernest Almer Heasman, was a carpenter who fought in World War I. His sister Alberta married John Andrews, a plumber; they moved first to Conneaut, then to Indiana, and finally to Inyo County, California (near Death Valley). His sister, Fannie, who was a weaver in Cobourg, married David Reid, a car finisher from England; they lived in Cobourg and later moved to Toronto.

Frederick Keith Heasman (1898-1960)

Frederick Keith "Keith" Heasman (1898-1960) -- nicknamed "Wimp" by friends and family -- married Marion Katherine Rogers (1898-1992) in Conneaut, Ohio, in 1919. They had one child, Patricia Ann, in 1924.

Both Keith and his brother Darrell Esmond "Red" Heasman (1901-1954) worked at Heasman's Grocery Store, which was originally located on State Street and later on Main and Mill Streets in Conneaut. According to Red's wife, Laura, the brothers "carried on the business having learned

Introduction

the business from youth. Frederick Keith learned to be manager of the grocery department and Darrell Esmond learned to run the meat department and was a first class meat cutter and manager of the meat department."

The three-story Heasman building on Main and Mill Streets had retail stores on the first floor, apartments on the second floor, and a ballroom on the third floor. Red and Laura lived in one of the apartments and Keith and his wife Marion lived in a home behind the grocery store built by F.H. Heasman. Red and Keith managed the property and worked at their grocery store until they died in 1954 and 1960 respectively. The Heasman building was demolished in 1964 to make room for a Kroger supermarket. The old Heasman Block is currently occupied by a Rite Aid pharmacy.

Maps

Origin Map for Kerr (Ireland) and Heasman (England)

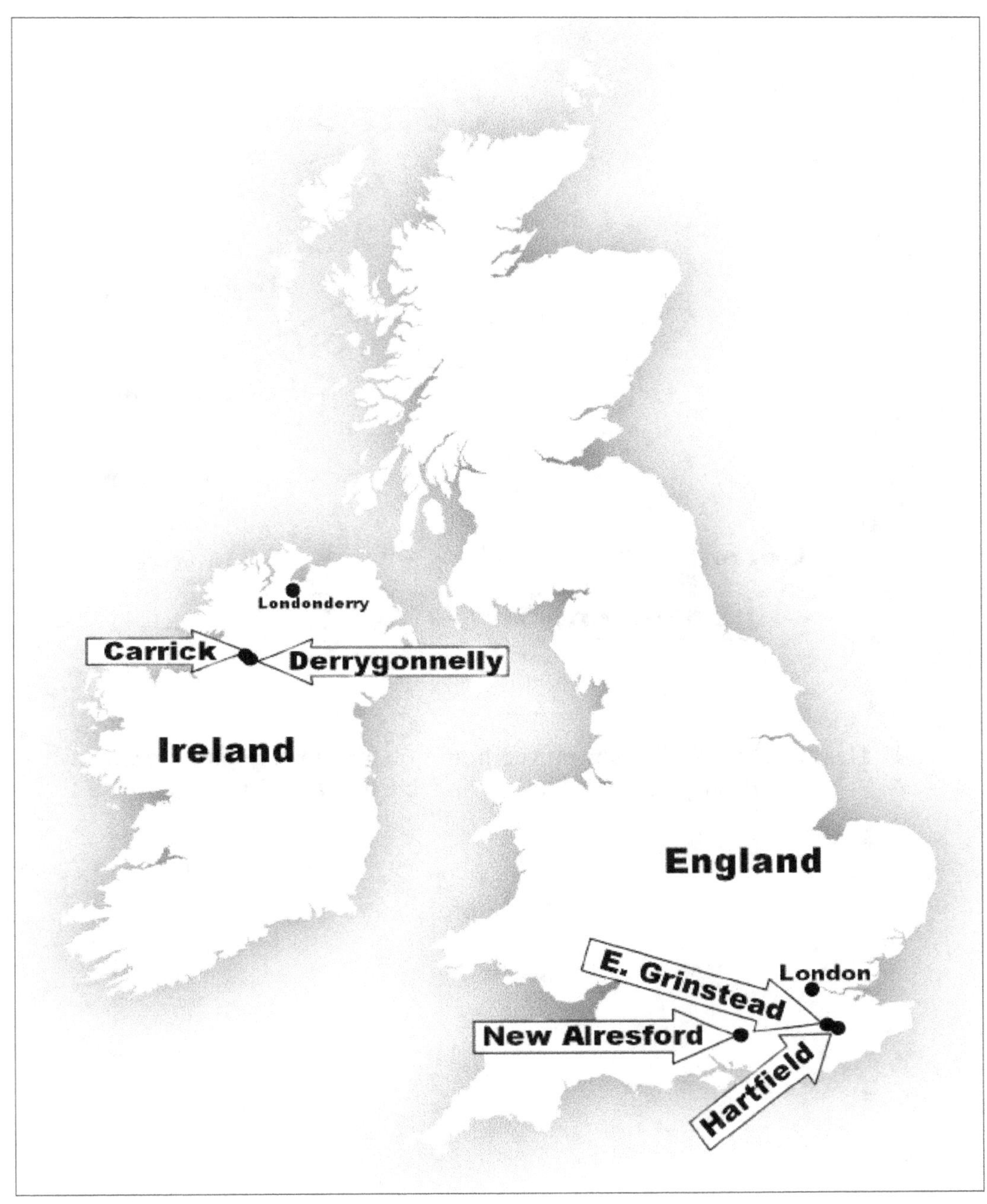

Immigrant Andrew Kerr moved from Carrick to Derrygonnelly, Ireland, before he and his family moved to Canada. Immigrant Thomas Heasman moved from Hartfield to New Alresford, England, before he and his family moved to Canada.

Maps

The Heasmans and Kerrs in the USA and Canada

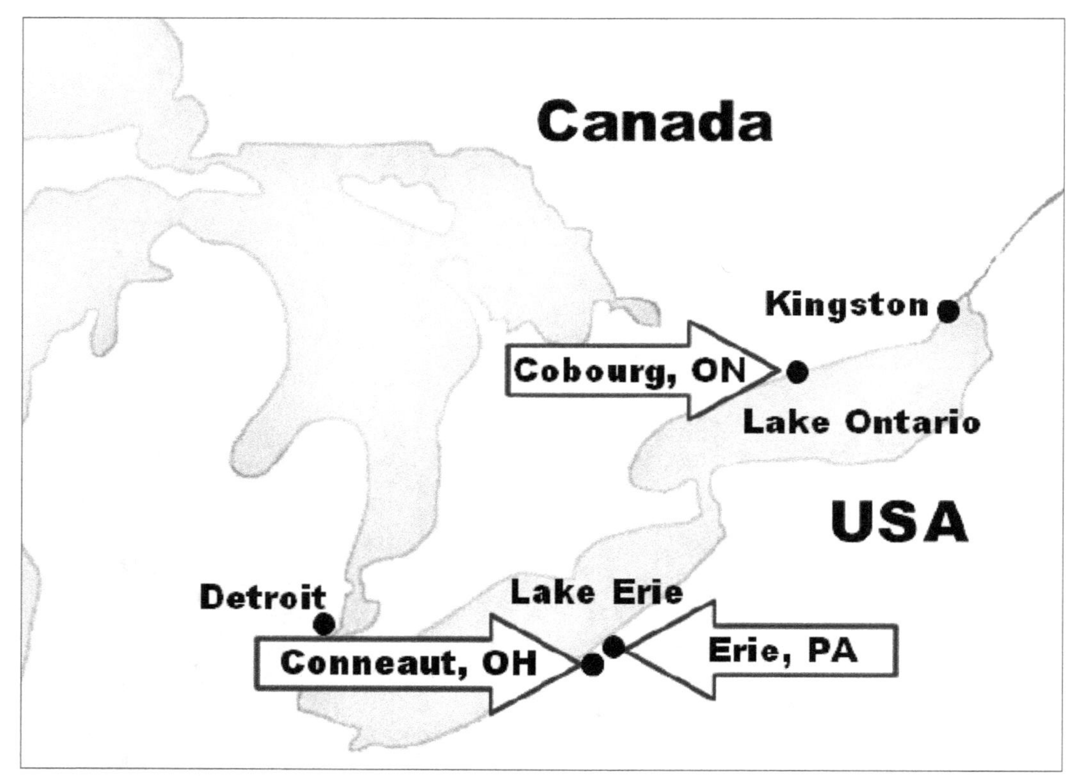

F.H. Heasman and Nellie Kerr moved from Cobourg, Ontario, to Erie County, Pennsylvania, before moving to Conneaut, Ohio.

Line of Descent from Great-Grandfather Samuel Heasman

First Generation

1. Samuel Heasman, son of **James Heasman** and **Elizabeth Turk,** was baptized on 9 Jun 1799 in Saint Mary the Virgin Church, Hartfield, Sussex, England[1] and was buried on 28 Feb 1855 in East Grinstead, Sussex, England.[2]

> General Notes: Samuel Heasman was an agricultural laborer. He lived with his wife and children in a cottage at Graddock's Pit Farm at Graddock's Pit Wood. Graddock's Pit, also called Cabbagestalk, lies between Ten Acre Wood and Paternoster Wood in West Hartfield. His brothers Thomas and Henry lived next door with his in-laws in the 1830s and 1840s.

Noted events in his life were:
- Occupation: agricultural laborer, 1841, Graddock's Pit, Hartfield, Sussex, England.[3]
- Occupation: agricultural laborer, 1851, Graddock's Pit, Hartfield, Sussex, England.[4]

Samuel married **Sarah Shoebridge,** daughter of **Jesse Shoebridge**[6] and **Karen "Carey" Weller,** on 2 Oct 1824 in Saint Swithuns, East Grinstead, Sussex, England.[5] Sarah was baptized on 20 Apr 1806 in Hartfield, Sussex, England[7] and died circa Feb 1872 in Sussex, England.[8]

Noted events in her life were:
- Resided: at Graddock's Pit farm, 1841, Hartfield, Sussex, England.[3]
- Resided: at Graddock's Pit farm, 1851, Hartfield, Sussex, England.[4]
- Resided: at Marsh Green, 1861, Hartfield, Sussex, England.[9]

Children from this marriage were:

+ 2 F   i.   **Harriett Heasman** was baptized on 2 Oct 1825 in Hartfield, Sussex, England,[10] died on 4 Feb 1866, and was buried on 4 Feb 1866 in Withyham, Sussex, England.[5]

> Harriett married **George Friend** (b. 1822, d. circa Nov 1883) on 9 Apr 1848 in Saint Michaels Church, Withyham, Sussex, England.[5]

+ 3 F   ii.   **Philadelphia Heasman** was baptized on 29 Mar 1829 in Hartfield, Sussex, England[11] and died circa Feb 1903 in East Grinstead, Sussex, England.[11]

> Philadelphia married **Thomas Groombridge** (c. 5 Mar 1826, d. 1872) on 26 Apr 1851 in Withyham, Sussex, England.[1]

> Philadelphia next married **William Neve** (b. 1833, d. about Nov 1904) on 18 Jan 1873 in Saint John, Crowborough, Sussex, England.[12]

+ 4 F   iii.   **Jane Heasman** was baptized on 30 Oct 1831 in Hartfield, Sussex, England[10] and died circa Feb 1909 in Sevenoaks, Kent, England.[11]

> Jane married **Michael Heasman** (b. 1827, d. circa Aug 1909) on 6 Apr 1854 in Saint Michaels Church, Withyham, Sussex, England.[12]

5 M   iv.   **Jesse Heasman** was baptized on 22 Jun 1834 in Hartfield, Sussex, England.[13]

Noted events in his life were:
- Resided: 1841, Graddock's Pit, Hartfield, Sussex, England.[3]
- Occupation: farm laborer at Graddocks Pit, 1851, Hartfield, Sussex, England.[4]

6 F   v.   **Mary Ann Heasman** was baptized on 25 Sep 1836 in Saint Mary the Virgin

Line of Descent from Great-Grandfather Samuel Heasman

Church, Hartfield, Sussex, England.[10]

Noted events in her life were:
* Resided: at Graddocks Pit, 1841, Hartfield, Sussex, England.[3]

* Occupation: servant at Graddocks Pit, 1851, Hartfield, Sussex, England.[4]

+ 7 M vi. **Thomas Heasman** was born on 20 Feb 1839 in Hartfield, Sussex, England,[14] was baptized on 24 Mar 1839 in Saint Mary the Virgin Church, Hartfield, Sussex, England,[1] and died on 17 Apr 1916 in Cobourg, Northumberland, Ontario, Canada.[14]

    Thomas married **Emily "Emma" Stubbs** (b. 30 Nov 1842, d. 19 Mar 1928) on 16 Dec 1865 in Ropley, Hampshire, England.[15]

+ 8 F vii. **Ann Heasman** was baptized on 9 Jan 1842 in Saint Mary the Virgin Church, Hartfield, Sussex, England[10] and died circa Aug 1920 in East Grinstead, Sussex, England.[11]

    Ann married **Edward Harman** (b. 1838, buried 20 Mar 1865) on 20 Apr 1861 in Saint Bartholomews Church, Burstow, Surrey, England.[16]

    Ann next married **Richard Payne** (b. 1838) on 26 Oct 1867 in East Grinstead, Sussex, England.[12]

9 F viii. **Hannah Heasman** was born circa Feb 1845 in Hartfield, Sussex, England,[17] was baptized on 16 Jan 1848 in Saint Mary the Virgin Church, Hartfield, Sussex, England,[10] and died in 1891 in Kensington, London, England.[11]

Noted events in her life were:
* Resided: at Graddocks Pit, 1851, Hartfield, Sussex, England.[4]

* Resided: at Marsh Green, 1861, Hartfield, Sussex, England.[9]

* Occupation: servant in the home of Frederich Diamant, 1871, Deptford, Saint Paul, London, England.[18]

* Occupation: Hospital supervisory nurse at Saint Thomas Hospital, 1881, Lambeth, London, England.[19]

10 F ix. **Emily Heasman** was born in 1848 in Hartfield, Sussex, England[9] and was baptized on 16 Jan 1848 in Saint Mary the Virgin Church, Hartfield, Sussex, England.[1]

Noted events in her life were:
* Occupation: servant for Learoyd family, 1871, Tunbridge Wells, Tunbridge, Kent, England.[18]

Line of Descent from Great-Grandfather Samuel Heasman

Second Generation (Children)

2. Harriett Heasman *(Samuel [1])* was baptized on 2 Oct 1825 in Hartfield, Sussex, England,[10] died on 4 Feb 1866, and was buried on 4 Feb 1866 in Withyham, Sussex, England.[5]

   Noted events in her life were:
   - Resided: at Blackham, 1851, Withyham, Sussex, England.[4] `

   - Resided: on Balls Green, 1861, Withyham, Sussex, England.[9]

Harriett married **George Friend,** son of **Robert Friend,** on 9 Apr 1848 in Saint Michaels Church, Withyham, Sussex, England.[5] George was born in 1822 in Lingfield, Surrey, England[4] and died circa Nov 1883 in East Grinstead, Sussex, England.[11]

   Noted events in his life were:
   - Occupation: agricultural laborer, 1851, East Grinstead, Sussex, England.[4]

   - Resided: 1881, Withyham, Sussex, England.[19]

Children from this marriage were:
   11   F   i.   **Emily Friend** was born in 1849 in Withyham, Sussex, England.

   12   M   ii.   **Thomas Friend**[9] was born in 1851 in Withyham, Sussex, England.[9]

   13   F   iii.   **Jane Friend**[9] was born in 1853 in Withyham, Sussex, England.[9]

   14   M   iv.   **Jessie Friend**[9] was born in 1856 in East Grinstead, Sussex, England.[9]

   15   F   v.   **Mary Friend**[9] was born in 1859 in Withyham, Sussex, England.[9]

3. Philadelphia Heasman *(Samuel [1])* was baptized on 29 Mar 1829 in Hartfield, Sussex, England[11] and died circa Feb 1903 in East Grinstead, Sussex, England.[11]

   Noted events in her life were:
   - Resided: 1841, Graddock's Pit, Hartfield, Sussex, England.[3]

   - Occupation: servant, 1851, Hartfield, Sussex, England.[4]

   - Resided: 1881, Crowborough, Sussex, England.[19]

   - Resided: on Marden's Hill, 1891, Crowborough, Sussex, England.[20]

   - Resided: on Mardens Hill, 1901, Withyham, Sussex, England.[21]

Philadelphia married **Thomas Groombridge,** son of **James Groombridge**[10] and **Rebecca Carr,**[10] on 26 Apr 1851 in Withyham, Sussex, England.[1] Thomas was baptized on 5 Mar 1826 in Saint Michaels Church, Withyham, Sussex, England,[10] died in 1872 in East Grinstead, Sussex, England,[11] and was buried on 17 Jul 1872 in Withyham, Sussex, England.[5]

Children from this marriage were:
   16   F   i.   **Ann Groombridge**[9] was born in 1852 in Withyham, Sussex, England.[9]

   17   F   ii.   **Fanny Groombridge** was born in 1856 in Withyham, Sussex, England.[22]

   18   M   iii.   **James Groombridge** was born in 1860 in Hartfield, Sussex, England.[23]

   19   M   iv.   **George Samuel Groombridge** was born in 1862 in Withyham, Sussex, England.[22]

   20   F   v.   **Elizabeth Groombridge** was born in 1865 in Withyham, Sussex, England.[18]

Line of Descent from Great-Grandfather Samuel Heasman

21 M   vi. **Jesse Groombridge** was born in 1871 in Withyham, Sussex, England[11] and was baptized on 28 May 1871 in Withyham, Sussex, England.[10]

Philadelphia next married **William Neve** on 18 Jan 1873 in Saint John, Crowborough, Sussex, England.[12] William was born in 1833 in Withyham, Sussex, England,[24] was baptized on 21 Apr 1833 in Saint Michaels Church, Withyham, Sussex, England,[10] and died about Nov 1904 in East Grinstead, Sussex, England.[11]

Noted events in his life were:
- Resided: at Friars Gate, Withyham, Sussex, England.[9]

4. Jane Heasman *(Samuel [1])* was baptized on 30 Oct 1831 in Hartfield, Sussex, England[10] and died circa Feb 1909 in Sevenoaks, Kent, England.[11]

Noted events in her life were:
- Resided: 1841, Graddock's Pit, Hartfield, Sussex, England.[3]
- Resided: at Blackham, 1861, Withyham, Sussex, England.[9]
- Resided: at Walters Green, 1881, Penshurst, Kent, England.[19]
- Resided: at Walters Green, 1891, Penshurst, Kent, England.[25]
- Resided: at Walters Green, 1901, Penshurst, Kent, England.[21]

Jane married **Michael Heasman,** son of **Samuel Heasman**[10] and **Mary Wise,**[10] on 6 Apr 1854 in Saint Michaels Church, Withyham, Sussex, England.[12] Michael was born in 1827 in Hartfield, Sussex, England,[9] was baptized on 29 Aug 1827 in Hartfield, Sussex, England,[10] and died circa Aug 1909 in Sevenoaks, Kent, England.[11]

Noted events in his life were:
- Occupation: agricultural laborer, 1861, Withyham, Sussex, England.[9]
- Resided: at Walters Green, 1901, Penshurst, Kent, England.[21]

Children from this marriage were:
  22 F   i. **Fanny Heasman** was born in 1858.[9]

  23 F   ii. **Sarah A. Heasman** was born in 1861 in Withyham, Sussex, England.[9]

  24 F   iii. **Emily Heasman** was born in 1868 in Withyham, Sussex, England.[19]

  25 F   iv. **Agnes Heasman** was born in 1871 in Withyham, Sussex, England.[19]

7. Thomas Heasman *(Samuel [1])* was born on 20 Feb 1839 in Hartfield, Sussex, England,[14] was baptized on 24 Mar 1839 in Saint Mary the Virgin Church, Hartfield, Sussex, England,[1] and died on 17 Apr 1916 in Cobourg, Northumberland, Ontario, Canada.[14]

General Notes:

Thomas Heasman left his home in Hartfield, England where he was a farm laborer and moved fifty miles west to Ropley village near the town of Alresford (pronounced "Alsford"), Hampshire County (abbreviated "Hants"). He worked for Mid-Hants Railway Company, which in 1861 had started work on a railway through Ropley connecting to London. The new railway, which was completed in 1865, allowed watercress farmers in the area to ship fresh watercress to London. A portion of the railway is still open and operates as the "Watercress Line."

In the early 1870s, the government of Ontario, Canada distributed flyers to workers in England encouraging immigration. Thomas Heasman and his family boarded a sailing vessel bound for Quebec in 1873. The trip took six weeks, and upon arrival they moved to Cobourg, Ontario, a small town southwest of

Line of Descent from Great-Grandfather Samuel Heasman

Kingston on the north shore of Lake Ontario.

Thomas Heasman found employment as a railroad worker with the Grand Trunk Railway. The original Grand Trunk line was completed in 1856 and connected Montreal to Toronto. In 1873 the Grand Trunk Railway Company continued to extend the line and began converting existing track to the "Standard" gauge. Thomas Heasman worked for the railroad for a time, then took up farming and later became a milk dealer in Cobourg, Canada.

Noted events in his life were:
- Resided: 1841, Graddock's Pit, Hartfield, Sussex, England. [3]

- Occupation: farm laborer, 1851, Graddock's Pit, Hartfield, Sussex, England. [4]

- Occupation: railway platelayer (track maintenance), 1871, New Alresford, Hampshire, England. [18]

- Immigration: 1873, Canada.

- Occupation: laborer, 1881, Cobourg, Northumberland, Ontario, Canada. [26]

- Religion: Bible Christian (Wesleyan Methodist), 1881. [26]

- Occupation: farmer, 1891, Cobourg, Northumberland, Ontario, Canada. [27]

- Religion: 1891, Methodist. [27]

- Occupation: milk dealer, 1901, Cobourg, Northumberland, Ontario, Canada. [28]

- Resided: 1911, Cobourg, Northumberland, Ontario, Canada. [29]

- Cause of death: suddenly from heart disease.

Thomas married **Emily "Emma" Stubbs,** daughter of **Henry Stubbs** and **Sarah Paice,** on 16 Dec 1865 in Ropley, Hampshire, England. [15] Emily "Emma" was born on 30 Nov 1842 in Ropley, Hampshire, England, [30] was baptized on 11 Dec 1842 in Ropley, Hampshire, England, [7] died on 19 Mar 1928 in York, Ontario, Canada, [31] and was buried on 21 Mar 1928 in Cobourg, Northumberland, Ontario, Canada. [32]

Emma Stubbs

General Notes: As a teenager Emma Stubbs worked as a servant at the home of retired navy commander Lt. Charles Batten in the East End Villa of West Meon, Hampshire, England. The Battans had two servants: Emma. the cook, and Ann Upsdale, the house maid. Emma married Thomas Heasman in 1865 and immigrated to Canada with her husband and three children in 1873. They settled in Cobourg where they had three more children. After Thomas died in 1916 she moved in with her son Frank in New Liskeard, Ontario.

Noted events in her life were:
- Occupation: cook in the Charles Batten home, 1861, West Meon, Hampshire, England. [9]

- Resided: 1871, New Alresford, Hampshire, England. [18]

- Resided: 1891, Cobourg, Northumberland, Ontario, Canada. [27]

- Resided: 1911, Cobourg, Northumberland, Ontario, Canada. [29]

- Boarder Crossing: 15 Jun 1918, Buffalo, Erie, New York. [33]

- Resided: 1921, New Liskeard, Temiskaming, Ontario, Canada. [34]

Line of Descent from Great-Grandfather Samuel Heasman

Children from this marriage were:

26 M   i. **Frank Heasman** was born on 23 Oct 1867 in New Alresford, Hampshire, England.[35]

Noted events in his life were:

• Resided: 1871, New Alresford, Hampshire, England.[18]

• Immigration: to Canada, 1873.[29]

• Witness: marriage of John Watt and Mary Ann Mitchell, 11 Oct 1887, Northumberland, Ontario, Canada.[36]

• Occupation: loom tuner, 1891, Ontario, Canada.[27]

• Religion: donation to Methodist missionaries, 1900, Cobourg, Northumberland, Ontario, Canada.[37]

• Resided: 1901, Cobourg, Northumberland, Ontario, Canada.[28] Worked as a weaver.

• Fact: from local hstory book, circa 1905, New Liskeard, Temiskaming, Ontario, Canada.[38] "All the while, one block west of the Grand Union, Frank Heasman's Grocery prepares a penny confectionery counter for the coming school year."

• Advertisement: in Agricultural Temiskaming magazine, 1910.[39]

Heasman's General Store, One of the most Popular Stores of the North
We carry Groceries, Chinaware, Dry Goods, Fancy Goods, Boots and Shoes, Toys.
Whitewood Ave., New Liskeard

• Resided: 1911, Nipissing, Ontario, Canada.[29]

• Newspaper Article: 19 Apr 1915, Barrie, Ontario, Canada.[40]

The New Liskeard Herald says that Frank Heasman (formerly a Barrie grocer) has bought the old Imperial Bank block in that town and will make big changes and improvements in the premises before moving in.

• Magazine Article: in Canadian Grocer, 7 Apr 1916.[41]

Novel Contrivance in Window
    Frank Heasman, of New Liskeard, Ont., recently reopened his new store after a disastrous fire that visited the block in which he was a short time ago. Mr. Heasman has a number of novel ideas which he puts into practice in his store. One is a method of his own in window display. Instead of the ordinary window with wide seat and constructed flat or at an incline he has a number of small neat tables, each with a flexible top. These tops can be raised to any desired angle, and then filled with whatever goods it is wished to show. The tables are arranged across in front of the window, and when dressed give a neat and attractive display. The body of the table underneath the top has a receptacle about six inches deep, and in this, there is kept ready for handing out a quantity of the articles on display on the table. If, for instance, there are oranges shown, there will be in the drawer below paper bags, each containing a dozen or half dozen of the same quality orange. Another contrivance he has is one that was described in the Canadian Grocer some time ago. It is a method of keeping frost off the show window. Mr. Heasman's construction is, however, a little different from the one referred to. His is the double window half way up, but instead of the cross piece for the

Line of Descent from Great-Grandfather Samuel Heasman

outside glass to rest against, he has a piece of thick rubber between the two glasses at the top of the outside or inside, whichever side the half window is placed. This being also made air tight around the sides and bottom; it effectually keeps the window from frosting.

- Resided: 1921, New Liskeard, Temiskaming, Ontario, Canada. [34]

- Resided: 1924, Toronto, Ontario, Canada. [42]

> Frank married **Ann Curtis,** daughter of **Samuel Curtis**[44] and **Elizabeth Scott,** in 1891 in Cobourg, Northumberland, Ontario, Canada. [43] Ann was born on 30 Jun 1868 in Parkhill, Middlesex, Ontario, Canada, [45] died on 6 Jul 1929 in Toronto, Ontario, Canada, [44] and was buried in Cobourg, Northumberland, Ontario, Canada. [44]

Noted events in her life were:
- Resided: 1901, Northumberland, Ontario, Canada. [28]

- Resided: 1911, Nipissing, Ontario, Canada. [29]

- Resided: 1921, New Liskeard, Temiskaming, Ontario, Canada. [34]

27 M   ii. **Frederick Huston "F. H." Heasman**[46] was born on 29 Oct 1869 in New Alresford, Hampshire, England, [47] died on 6 May 1952 in Conneaut, Ashtabula, Ohio, [46] and was buried in Glenwood Cemetery, Conneaut, Ashtabula, Ohio.

F.H. Heasman

> General Notes: F.H. Heasman was born in England, immigrated with his family to Canada at the age of four, and immigrated to America at the age of twenty-five. He raised his family in Conneaut, Ohio, where he became a noted merchant and entrepreneur best known for his property called the Heasman Block and for Heasman's Grocery. He married twice: first to Nellie Kerr with whom he had his children Keith and Darrell, and second to Gertrude Zundel. [48]

Noted events in his life were:
- Immigration: 1873, Canada. [49]

- Occupation: woolen weaver, 1891, Cobourg, Northumberland, Ontario, Canada. [27]

- Occupation: railroad worker, barge worker, tugboat worker, before 1894, Canada. [50]

- Immigration: 1894, Pennsylvania. [51]

- Resided: 1894, Harris, Ontario, Canada. [52]

- Occupation: merchant, 1900, Conneaut, Ashtabula, Ohio. [53] Residing with his wife Nellie, his brother William, and his child Keith.

- Resided: at 420 Buffalo Street, 1908, Conneaut, Ashtabula, Ohio. [54]

- Occupation: store owner, 1910, Conneaut, Ashtabula, Ohio. [55] He was a partner in Union Mercantile Company. He lived at 452 State St.

- Resided: at 378 1/2 Main Street, 1912, Conneaut, Ashtabula, Ohio. [54]

- Occupation: owner, Heasman Grocery, 382-394 Main St., 1916, Conneaut, Ashtabula, Ohio. [56]

Line of Descent from Great-Grandfather Samuel Heasman

- Resided: Heasman Block (former Baldwin Block), 1916, Conneaut, Ashtabula, Ohio. [56] In 1911, F.H. bought a grand, multi-story building on the northeast corner of Main and Mill Street -- formerly the Baldwin Block -- where he opened a dry goods store and a grocery store.

- Article: marriage notice in Conneaut News-Herald, 16 Sep 1919, Conneaut, Ashtabula, Ohio.[57]

Miss Zundel Weds Mr. F.H. Heasman

A very quiet wedding which took their many friends completely by surprise, occurred last Saturday evening when Miss Gertrude E. Zundel, daughter of Mrs. Emma Zundel, 149 Evergreen street, was united in marriage to Mr. Fred H. Heasman, well known Conneaut business man.

The wedding took place at the parsonage of the First Methodist church of this city, Rev. J. H. Blackburn, pastor of the church, conducting the ceremony which was a very simple one, the bride and groom having no attendants.

Mr. and Mrs. Heasman, accompanied by Darrell Heasman, left Saturday night for a ten days' motor trip to Canada. Upon their return they will be at home in the Heasman block, Main street.

The newly-married couple are both well known here and have many friends who will wish to extend their heartiest congratulations. Mrs. Heasman is especially well known because of her exceptional musical ability, while Mr. Heasman has been one of Conneaut's most active business men.

- Occupation: grocery store owner, 1920, Conneaut, Ashtabula, Ohio. [58]

- Bio: From History of Ashtabula County, 1924. [42]

Fred H. Heasman, a progressive and enterprising business man of Conneaut, was born in England, Oct. 29, 1869, and is a son of Thomas and Anna (Stubbs) Heasman.

The Heasman family came to Canada from England in 1872, locating at Kingston, where Thomas Heasman engaged in railroad building. He is now deceased. His wife lives at Toronto, Canada, and is 82 years of age. There were six children in the Heasman family: Frank lives in Toronto, Can.; Fred H., the subject of this sketch; Fannie married David Reid, lives in Toronto, Can.; William, lives at Moose Jaw, Saskatchewan; Alberta, married J. S. Andrews, lives in Los Angeles, Calif.; and Ernest lives in Canada. He served throughout the World War with the Canadian forces and has since been an invalid.

Fred H. Heasman was reared and educated in Canada, coming to the United States when 19 years of age, locating first in Erie, Pa. In 1896 he went to West Springfield, Pa., and engaged in the general merchandise business with W. G. Walker, under the firm name Walker and Heasman. In 1898 Mr. Heasman came to Conneaut and engaged in his present business. He has been located in his present building, 382-394 Main Street, since 1911. He is a general merchant and has an extensive business.

Mr. Heasman was married the first time to Miss Nellie Kerr, who died in 1918. To this union two children were born: Frederick Keith, and Darrell, who are both in business with their father. Frederick Keith Heasman was married to Miss Marion Rodgers, a native of Conneaut. Two and one-half years after the death of his first wife, Fred H. Heasman was married to Miss Gertrude Zundel, a native of Pittsburgh, Pa.

Mr. Heasman is a Republican and a member of the Rotary Club. He and his family are members of the Methodist Church, and are held in high esteem in their community.

Line of Descent from Great-Grandfather Samuel Heasman

- Occupation: manager of general store, The Heasman Co., 380-386 Main (Heasmans Block), 1930, Conneaut, Ashtabula, Ohio.[59]
- Resided: 378 Main, 1940, Conneaut, Ashtabula, Ohio.[60]
- Bio: Ashtabula County History, Then and Now, 1985.[61]

Fred H. Heasman was born in Alsford Hans [Alresford, Hants], England. He came over in a sailing boat, a six week trip and landed in Quebec, Canada, and from there to Kingston. His father was building the Great Trunk Railroad from Canada to Erie, Penn. He lived in Canada 47 years.

Fred H. Heasman sailed two years on what was a river tug.... The tug towed to Lake Huron, Sault St. Marie.... He was 19 years of age. In 1895 he came to the United States and worked in the Boston Store in Erie, Penn.

Times were hard and when 11 years old he worked in a small grocery in Michigan. Fred worked for Rushbrook Tug, Wales, towing lumber barges to Tonawanda and Black Rock, NY, Oswego, St. Clair River. He then worked for The Eaton Company, Toronto, Can., then worked for a grocer in North Bay, Ontario, married and lived two years in Canada. He then came to the United States and opened a grocery store in West Springfield, Penn, and then in Conneaut, Ohio where he was in business the rest of his life. He died in 1952.

His first wife, Nellie, died and he remarried two years later to Gertrude M. Zundel, who was a friend of the family and a bookkeeper in the Heasman Grocery and Meat Company, 378-384 Main St. Two sons were born who carried on the business having learned the business from youth. Frederick Keith learned to be manager of the grocery department and Darrell Esmond learned to run the meat department and was a first class meat cutter and manager of the meat department.

Frederick Keith was married to Marion Rogers Heasman Gruber (now) and they had one daughter, Patricia (Eagles). She and her husband, James, have one daughter, not married, who is in a nursing career and lives in California.

Darrell Esmond Heasman married Laura Jane Hogle and has one daughter, Mary Ann, who married Joseph Loren Burns. They have three children, James Joseph, Cynthia Sue and Michael Christopher. Mary Ann and Joseph Loren have three grandchildren, Kristen, Scott, and Christine.

Mary Ann and Joseph Loren Burns live in Bellvue, Ohio. Their son, James, and family also live in Bellvue. Their daughter, Cynthia Sue, and family live in Hillsboro, Ohio. She is married to Richard D. Eigel, a meat inspector for the government. Cynthia Sue teaches music (band and choir) in the Hillsboro High School.

Frederick Keith was born in 1899 and died in 1960 (age 61). Darrell Esmond was born Feb 12, 1901 and died Sept. 18, 1954 (age 52).

Mary Ann and Joseph Loren's son, Michael C., is a junior in high school, being born the year that his older brother, James Joseph, was graduating from High School.

Darrell and Laura built a summer home at 853 Lakeview Ave. in Conneaut, Ohio, where Laura still lives since her husband's death, to build up Social Security, as they did not have Social Security when her husband was living. The Heasman Meat and Grocery Store was torn down in July, 1962, to make room to build the Kroger Store, which is now vacant.

Marian Heasman Gruber, is widow of her second husband, Henry Gruber, who formerly owned "The Syndicate," a woman's apparel store. She is now living in Ashtabula County Nursing Home in Kingsville, Ohio.

- Bio: Patricia Heasman oral history, 2002.[48]

F.H. came to Canada from England -- six weeks on a sail boat -- and landed in Quebec,

Line of Descent from Great-Grandfather Samuel Heasman

then moved to Kingston, Ontario. F.H. and his father helped build the Grand Trunk RR between Ontario and Erie. His first job was in a grocery at 11 years, at 19 years sailed on river tugs for two years towing barges to Lake Huron, and then worked at Wales, Ontario on the tug Walter Rushbrook, ferrying boats up the St. Clair River. He also worked as a lumberjack, and at Eaton Department Store in Toronto. There he met Charlie Crombie, both married and lived in Toronto for about 2 years, before coming to the States. In 1895 Fred and Nellie Heasman moved to Erie, Pennsylvania. F.H. worked in a carpet department store in Erie, Pennsylvania, called the Boston Store. He opened a grocery store in West Springfield, Pennsylvania. Charlie Crombie opened a grocery on State Street in Conneaut (across from the now Silver Diner). Fred bought the Baldwin Block on the corner of Main & Mill Streets in Conneaut and opened the Heasman Grocery and Meat Company in about 1900. His sons Frederick Keith and Darrel Esmond both worked there.

Frederick Huston "F. H." married **Elinor "Nellie" Kerr,** daughter of **Andrew Kerr** and **Jane Allingham,** on 7 Aug 1894 in Corry, Erie, Pennsylvania.[52] Elinor "Nellie" was born on 19 Mar 1870 in Baltimore, Hamilton, Northumberland, Ontario, Canada,[62] died on 30 May 1918 in Conneaut, Ashtabula, Ohio,[63] and was buried on 2 Jun 1918 in Glenwood Cemetery, Conneaut, Ashtabula, Ohio.[46]

Nellie Kerr

Marriage Notes: She and her sister Jennie were married one day apart in Corry, Erie, Pennsylvania.

General Notes: Nellie Kerr's parents and eldest sister were born in Ireland and Nellie was born in Canada. She moved with two sisters, Jennie and Lottie, from their farm in Hamilton Township, Ontario, to nearby Cobourg where she worked as a dressmaker. Nellie married F.H. Heasman in Erie County, Pennsylvania and settled in Conneaut, Ohio. They had two children.

Noted events in her life were:
- Resided: 1881, Hamilton Township, Northumberland, Ontario, Canada.[26]

- Religion: Methodist, 1891.[27]

- Resided: lodger, 1891, Cobourg, Northumberland, Ontario, Canada.[27]

- Resided: 1894, Erie, Erie, Pennsylvania.[52]

- Resided: 1900, Conneaut, Ashtabula, Ohio.[53]

- Resided: at 452 State St., 1910, Conneaut, Ashtabula, Ohio.[55]

Line of Descent from Great-Grandfather Samuel Heasman

Frederick Huston "F. H." next married **Gertrude Zundel,** daughter of **Robert H. Zundel**[53] and **Emma V. Tucker,**[65] on 13 Sep 1919 in Conneaut, Ashtabula, Ohio.[64] Gertrude was born on 29 Aug 1885 in Pittsburgh, Allegheny, Pennsylvania[66] and died on 14 Jun 1972 in Conneaut, Ashtabula, Ohio.[67]

Gertrude Zundel

Noted events in her life were:

• Occupation: bookkeeper Heasman's Grocery.[68]

• Resided: 1900, Jamestown, Mercer, Pennsylvania.[53]

• Occupation: bookkeeper in department store, 1910, Conneaut, Ashtabula, Ohio.[49]

• Obituary: from Conneaut News-Herald, 14 Jun 1972, Conneaut, Ashtabula, Ohio.[69]

\----------

Mrs. Heasman

Funeral services for Mrs. Gertrude E. (Trudy) Heasman, 86, of 182 Mill St., will be held at the Thompson Funeral Home at 1 p.m. Saturday.

The Rev. Lawrence Miller, pastor, First United Methodist Church will officiate.

Burial will be in Glenwood Cemetery.

Friends may call at the funeral home from 2 to 4 p.m. and 7 to 9 p.m. Friday.

Born in Pittsburgh, Pa. Aug. 29, 1885, she was the daughter of Albert H. and Emma (Tupper) Zundahl. She had been a Conneaut resident since 1899 and was formerly associated with her husband for over 60 years in the former Heasman Grocery Store.

She was a lifetime member of the First United Methodist Church; a member of Sorosis I; Mystic Circle; E. Club; the WSCs of First United Methodist Church, and she served as secretary of the church for more than 40 years.

She is survived by two granddaughters, Mrs. James (Patricia) Eagles, and Mrs. J. Loren (Mary Ann) Burns, both of Conneaut; four great-grandchildren; two sisters, Mrs. Helen Boyle, Conneaut, with whom she made her home, and Mrs. Mabel Beymer, Chicago, Ill.

She was preceded in death by her husband, Fred, in 1952.

Mrs. Heasman died at 8 a.m. today in Brown Memorial Hospital where she had been admitted last Sunday. Her death was due complications of an extended illness.

\--------

Line of Descent from Great-Grandfather Samuel Heasman

28 F   iii. **Fannie Heasman** was born on 30 Jan 1872 in New Alresford, Hampshire, England,[27] died on 1 Feb 1942,[70] and was buried in Mount Pleasant Cemetery, Toronto, Ontario, Canada.[70]

Fannie Heasman

> General Notes: Fannie Heasman married David Reid, a "car finisher" born in England, They lived in Cobourg and later moved to Toronto. He was Presbyterian and she was a Methodist. She immigrated in 1873 and he in 1889.

Noted events in her life were:
- Immigration: 1873.[28]

- Occupation: woolen weaver, 1891, Cobourg, Northumberland, Ontario, Canada.[27]

- Resided: 1901, Northumberland, Ontario, Canada.[28]

- Resided: 1924, Toronto, Ontario, Canada.[42]

> Fannie married **David S. Reid,** son of **Gordon Reid**[43] and **Elizabeth Millar,**[43] on 10 Jun 1896 in Cobourg, Northumberland, Ontario, Canada.[43] David S. was born on 8 Mar 1865 in England,[70] died on 28 Jan 1949 in Toronto, Ontario, Canada,[70] and was buried in Mount Pleasant Cemetery, Toronto, Ontario, Canada.[70]

David Reid

Noted events in his life were:
- Occupation: car finisher.

- Immigration: to Canada, 1889.

29 M   iv. **William Heasman** was born on 16 May 1874 in Cobourg, Northumberland, Ontario, Canada,[71] died on 12 Feb 1969 in Victoria, British Columbia, Canada,[72] and was buried in Saanich, British Columbia, Canada.[72]

William Heasman

> General Notes: William Heasman was born in Canada and moved to Conneaut where he lived with his brother, F.H. Heasman. He moved to Moose Jaw, Saskatchewan, Canada, where he opened a millinery and women's fashion store in 1916. The store, operating as Heasman's since the 1940's at 304 Main St. North, was closed in 2004.

Noted events in his life were:
- Occupation: wool spinner, 1891, Cobourg, Northumberland, Ontario, Canada.[27]

- Occupation: clerk, 1900, Conneaut, Ashtabula, Ohio.[53]

Line of Descent from Great-Grandfather Samuel Heasman

- Resided: 1906, Moose Jaw, Saskatchewan, Canada. [73]

- Resided: 1949, Moose Jaw, Saskatchewan, Canada. [74]

- Retired: 1950, British Columbia, Canada. [72]

> William married **Annie Evaline Hart**,[72] daughter of **Charles E. Hart** and **Eva Ridley**. Annie Evaline was born on 9 Dec 1884 in Toronto, Ontario, Canada. [75]

> William next married **Margaret C. McCammon,** daughter of **John B. McCammon**[43] and **Eliza Jane Gewan**,[43] on 30 Apr 1901 in Toronto, York, Ontario, Canada.[43] Margaret C. was born in Nov 1875 in Ireland[76] and died circa 1950 in Moose Jaw, Saskatchewan, Canada.

Margaret McCammon

> General Notes: Worked in Heasman's Moose Jaw hat store.

Noted events in her life were:
- Immigration: 1887, Canada.[73]

- Resided: 1906, Moose Jaw, Saskatchewan, Canada. [73]

- Resided: 1949, Moose Jaw, Saskatchewan, Canada. [74]

30 F   v.   **Alberta Heasman** was born on 23 Jul 1878 in Cobourg, Northumberland, Ontario, Canada[27] and died in 1929 in California.[77]

Noted events in her life were:
- Emigrated: 1902, Canada.[58]

- Resided: 1910, Gary, Lake, Indiana.[49]

- Resided: 1920, Gary, Lake, Indiana.[58]

> Alberta married **John Shilby Andrews**,[43] son of **Martin Lewis Andrews**[43] and **Mary Wagner**,[43] on 11 Sep 1902 in Cobourg, Northumberland, Ontario, Canada.[43] John Shilby was born on 12 Sep 1880 in Adams, Indiana[78] and died on 15 Nov 1963 in Bishop, Inyo, California.[79]
>
> General Notes: He was a plumber.

31 M   vi. **Sgt. Ernest Almer "E.A." Heasman** was born on 13 Jun 1887 in Cobourg, Northumberland, Ontario, Canada.[80]

> General Notes: Earnest Heasman was a carpenter who served in World War I in the 39th Battalion of the Canadian forces overseas.
>
> Research Notes: It is said Ernest Heasman had a war injury and a related disability. His possible month of death is Feb 1859.

Noted events in his life were:
- Resided: 1891, Cobourg, Northumberland, Ontario, Canada.[27]

Line of Descent from Great-Grandfather Samuel Heasman

- Resided: 1901, Cobourg, Northumberland, Ontario, Canada. [28]

- Military: served 2 years on Cobourg Heavy Battery with rank of sargeant, before 1915. [81]

- Occupation: Carpenter, before 1915, Cobourg, Northumberland, Ontario, Canada. [81]

- Military: signed attestation for overseas expeditionay force in WWI, 1915. [81] He enlisted as a private in the 39th Battalion and his regimental number was 412379.

- Resided: 1921, Cobourg, Northumberland, Ontario, Canada. [34]

- Registered Voter: 1935, Northumberland, Ontario, Canada. [74]

- Registered Voter: 1957, Ontario, Canada. [74]

Ernest Almer "E.A." married **Lillian**. [34] Lillian was born about 1890. [34]

8. Ann Heasman *(Samuel [1])* was baptized on 9 Jan 1842 in Saint Mary the Virgin Church, Hartfield, Sussex, England [10] and died circa Aug 1920 in East Grinstead, Sussex, England. [11]

Noted events in her life were:
- Resided: at Graddocks Pit, 1851, Hartfield, Sussex, England. [4]

- Resided: at Homestall Cottage, 1881, Ashurst Wood, East Grinstead, Sussex, England. [19]

- Resided: at Homestall Cottage, 1891, Ashurst Wood, East Grinstead, Sussex, England. [25]

Ann married **Edward Harman, son of Edward Harman,** on 20 Apr 1861 in Saint Bartholomews Church, Burstow, Surrey, England. [16] Edward was born in 1838 [5] and was buried on 20 Mar 1865 in East Grinstead, Sussex, England. [5]

Children from this marriage were:
    32 M   i. **Jesse Harman** was born in 1863 in East Grinstead, Sussex, England. [18]

    33 M   ii. **Edward George Harman** was born in 1865 in Ashurst, Kent, England. [82]

Ann next married **Richard Payne** on 26 Oct 1867 in East Grinstead, Sussex, England. [12] Richard was born in 1838 in East Grinstead, Sussex, England. [19]

General Notes: He was a stockman and shepherd.

Children from this marriage were:
    34 M   i. **Richard Payne** was born in 1869 in East Grinstead, Sussex, England. [19]

    35 M   ii. **George Payne** was born in 1871 in East Grinstead, Sussex, England. [19]

    36 F   iii. **Rosina Payne** was born in 1872 in East Grinstead, Sussex, England. [19]

    37 F   iv. **William T. Payne** was born in 1876 in East Grinstead, Sussex, England. [19]

    38 F   v. **Edith Mary Payne** was born in 1879 in East Grinstead, Sussex, England. [19]

    39 F   vi. **Florence Payne** was born in 1881 in East Grinstead, Sussex, England. [19]

    40 M vii. **Charles Payne** was born in 1884 in East Grinstead, Sussex, England. [25]

<h1 align="center">Line of Descent from Great-Grandfather Henry Stubbs</h1>

First Generation

41. Henry Stubbs, son of **James Stubbs**[12] and **Mary Wateridge,** was baptized on 11 Aug 1816 in Ropley, Hampshire, England[83] and died in Apr 1891 in West Battersea, London, England. [84]

> General Notes: Henry Stubbs was a carter (delivered goods on an ox- or horse-drawn wagon) and agricultural laborer. The main agricultural crop in the area was watercress. He moved several times among neighboring villages. In his retirement he moved to London to live with his daughter, Frances.

Noted events in his life were:
- Occupation: agricultural laborer residing on North Street, 1841, Ropley, Hampshire, England.[3]
- Occupation: agricultural laborer residing at Ropley Soke, 1851, Ropley, Hampshire, England.[4]
- Occupation: carter, 1861, Ropley, Hampshire, England.[9]
- Occupation: agricultural laborer, 1871, Bishops Sutton, Alresford, Hampshire, England.[18] He lived on Ranscombe Farm which is on Barnetts Wood Lane between the villages of Bighton and Ropley
- Occupation: agricultural laborer residing at Sutton Wood Cottages, 1881, Bishops Sutton, Alresford, Hampshire, England.[19]
- Resided: widowed and living with his daughter Frances, 5 Apr 1891, West Battersea, London, England.[25]

Henry married **Sarah Paice,** daughter of **William Paice**[15] and **Hannah Aldred,** on 29 Feb 1840 in West Tisted, Hampshire, England.[15] Sarah was baptized on 17 Jan 1819 in West Tisted, Hampshire, England[10] and died circa May 1889 in Alresford, Hampshire, England. [11]

> Noted events in her life were:
> - Resided: on North Street, 1841, Ropley, Hampshire, England.[3]
> - Resided: 1851, Bishops Waltham, Hampshire, England.[4]
> - Resided: on Lymington Bottom, 1861, Ropley, Hampshire, England.[9]
> - Resided: on Ranscombe Farm, 1871, Bishops Sutton, Alresford, Hampshire, England.[18]
> - Resided: at Sutton Wood Cottages, 1881, Bishops Sutton, Alresford, Hampshire, England.[19]

Children from this marriage were:

+ 42   F   i. **Mary Ann Stubbs** was born circa 1840 in Ropley, Hampshire, England[86] and died circa Nov 1870 in Alton, Hampshire, England.[87]

> Mary Ann married **Edward Pullinger** (c. 8 Dec 1833, d. circa Nov 1905) on 12 Nov 1859 in Ropley, Hampshire, England.[15]

   43   M   ii. **Stubbs** was born about 1841.[3]

+ 44   F   iii. **Frances "Fanny" Stubbs** was baptized on 14 May 1841 in Ropley, Hampshire, England[21] and died in Mar 1924 in London, England.[32]

> Frances "Fanny" married **Charles Bricknell** (b. circa 1837) on 5 Jul 1862 in Ropley, Hampshire, England.[15]

+ 45   F   iv. **Emily "Emma" Stubbs** was born on 30 Nov 1842 in Ropley, Hampshire,

Line of Descent from Great-Grandfather Henry Stubbs

England,[30] was baptized on 11 Dec 1842 in Ropley, Hampshire, England,[7] died on 19 Mar 1928 in York, Ontario, Canada,[31] and was buried on 21 Mar 1928 in Cobourg, Northumberland, Ontario, Canada.[32]

Emily "Emma" married **Thomas Heasman** (b. 20 Feb 1839, d. 17 Apr 1916) on 16 Dec 1865 in Ropley, Hampshire, England.[15]

(Duplicate Line. See Person 7)

+ 46 F   v. **Elizabeth Stubbs** was baptized on 11 Aug 1844 in Ropley, Hampshire, England.[7]

Elizabeth married **William Redman** (b. circa 1841) on 12 Nov 1864 in Ropley, Hampshire, England.[89]

Line of Descent from Great-Grandfather Henry Stubbs

Second Generation (Children)

42. Mary Ann Stubbs *(Henry [1])* was born circa 1840 in Ropley, Hampshire, England[86] and died circa Nov 1870 in Alton, Hampshire, England.[87]

Noted events in her life were:
- Resided: 1851, Ropley, Hampshire, England.[4]

- Resided: 1861, Ropley, Hampshire, England.[9]

Mary Ann married **Edward Pullinger** on 12 Nov 1859 in Ropley, Hampshire, England.[15] Edward was baptized on 8 Dec 1833 in Ropley, Hampshire, England[1] and died circa Nov 1905 in Fareham, Hampshire, England.[8]

44. Frances "Fanny" Stubbs *(Henry [1])* was baptized on 14 May 1841 in Ropley, Hampshire, England[21] and died in Mar 1924 in London, England.[32]

Research Notes: She had 8 children.

Noted events in her life were:
- Occupation: house maid at Ropley Lodge, 1861, Ropley, Hampshire, England.[9]

- Resided: Church Street, 1871, Epsom, Surrey, England.[18]

- Resided: 38 Grove Road, 1881, Battersea, London, England.[19]

- Resided: 38 Este Road, 1891, Battersea, London, England.[25]

- Resided: 9 Falcon Terrace, 1901, Battersea, London, England.[21] Now the Asparagus Restaurant.

- Resided: 67 Lavender Rd., 1911, Battersea, London, England.[90]

Frances "Fanny" married **Charles Bricknell** on 5 Jul 1862 in Ropley, Hampshire, England.[15] Charles was born circa 1837 in Ropley, Hampshire, England.[90]

45. Emily "Emma" Stubbs *(Henry [1])* was born on 30 Nov 1842 in Ropley, Hampshire, England,[30] was baptized on 11 Dec 1842 in Ropley, Hampshire, England,[7] died on 19 Mar 1928 in York, Ontario, Canada,[31] and was buried on 21 Mar 1928 in Cobourg, Northumberland, Ontario, Canada.[32]

Emma Stubbs

General Notes: As a teenager Emma Stubbs worked as a servant at the home of retired navy commander Lt. Charles Batten in the East End Villa of West Meon, Hampshire, England. The Battans had two servants: Emma. the cook, and Ann Upsdale, the house maid. Emma married Thomas Heasman in 1865 and immigrated to Canada with her husband and three children in 1873. They settled in Cobourg where they had three more children. After Thomas died in 1916 she moved in with her son Frank in New Liskeard, Ontario.

Noted events in her life were:
- Occupation: cook in the Charles Batten home, 1861, West Meon, Hampshire, England.[9]

- Resided: 1871, New Alresford, Hampshire, England.[18]

- Resided: 1891, Cobourg, Northumberland, Ontario, Canada.[27]

- Resided: 1911, Cobourg, Northumberland, Ontario, Canada.[29]

Line of Descent from Great-Grandfather Henry Stubbs

- Boarder Crossing: 15 Jun 1918, Buffalo, Erie, New York. [33]

- Resided: 1921, New Liskeard, Temiskaming, Ontario, Canada. [34]

Emily "Emma" married **Thomas Heasman,** son of **Samuel Heasman** and **Sarah Shoebridge,** on 16 Dec 1865 in Ropley, Hampshire, England. [15] Thomas was born on 20 Feb 1839 in Hartfield, Sussex, England, [14] was baptized on 24 Mar 1839 in Saint Mary the Virgin Church, Hartfield, Sussex, England, [1] and died on 17 Apr 1916 in Cobourg, Northumberland, Ontario, Canada. [14]

General Notes:

Thomas Heasman left his home in Hartfield, England where he was a farm laborer and moved fifty miles west to Ropley village near the town of Alresford (pronounced "Alsford"), Hampshire County (abbreviated "Hants"). He worked for Mid-Hants Railway Company, which in 1861 had started work on a railway through Ropley connecting to London. The new railway, which was completed in 1865, allowed watercress farmers in the area to ship fresh watercress to London. A portion of the railway is still open and operates as the "Watercress Line."

In the early 1870s, the government of Ontario, Canada distributed flyers to workers in England encouraging immigration. Thomas Heasman and his family boarded a sailing vessel bound for Quebec in 1873. The trip took six weeks, and upon arrival they moved to Cobourg, Ontario, a small town southwest of Kingston on the north shore of Lake Ontario.

Thomas Heasman found employment as a railroad worker with the Grand Trunk Railway. The original Grand Trunk line was completed in 1856 and connected Montreal to Toronto. In 1873 the Grand Trunk Railway Company continued to extend the line and began converting existing track to the "Standard" gauge. Thomas Heasman worked for the railroad for a time, then took up farming and later became a milk dealer in Cobourg, Canada.

Noted events in his life were:
- Resided: 1841, Graddock's Pit, Hartfield, Sussex, England. [3]

- Occupation: farm laborer, 1851, Graddock's Pit, Hartfield, Sussex, England. [4]

- Occupation: railway platelayer (track maintenance), 1871, New Alresford, Hampshire, England. [18]

- Immigration: 1873, Canada.

- Occupation: laborer, 1881, Cobourg, Northumberland, Ontario, Canada. [26]

- Religion: Bible Christian (Wesleyan Methodist), 1881. [26]

- Occupation: farmer, 1891, Cobourg, Northumberland, Ontario, Canada. [27]

- Religion: 1891, Methodist. [27]

- Occupation: milk dealer, 1901, Cobourg, Northumberland, Ontario, Canada. [28]

- Resided: 1911, Cobourg, Northumberland, Ontario, Canada. [29]

- Cause of death: suddenly from heart disease.

(Duplicate Line. See Person 7)

46. Elizabeth Stubbs *(Henry [1])* was baptized on 11 Aug 1844 in Ropley, Hampshire, England. [7]

Noted events in her life were:
- Resided: 1851, Ropley, Hampshire, England. [4]

- Resided: 1871, Newton Valence, Hampshire, England. [18]

- Resided: 1891, Newton Valence, Hampshire, England. [25]

Line of Descent from Great-Grandfather Henry Stubbs

- Resided: 1901, Battersea, London, England.[21]
- Resided: 1911, Newton Valence, Hampshire, England.[90]

Elizabeth married **William Redman** on 12 Nov 1864 in Ropley, Hampshire, England.[89] William was born circa 1841.[15]

Line of Descent from Great-Grandfather George Kerr

First Generation

47. George Kerr,[14] son of **George Kerr** and **Margaret Eaton,** was born in Carrick, Fermanagh, Ireland[91] and was baptized on 13 Jan 1814 in Upper Inishmacsaint, Fermanagh, Ireland.[91]

> Christening Notes: Their church was in the village of Drumenagh, also called Church Hill. The church was built in 1688.

> General Notes: He is listed as landowner in Griffith Valuations, along with Robert, Thomas, and John of Carrick, who may have been his brothers or sons. He rented from Mervyn Edward Archdale, MP a house with yard and garden on Main street in Derrygonnelly, as well as a small parcel of land near John Allingham in Sandhill.

> Noted events in his life were:
> - Resided: at 44 Main St., 1862, Derrygonnelly, Fermanagh, Ireland.[92] House, yard, and garden leased from Edward Archdall. He also leased farmland from Archdall in Sandhill which is south and adjacent to Carrick.

George married **Jane** about 1835 in Ireland.[93]

Children from this marriage were:

+ 48 M   i. **Thomas Kerr**[28] was born on 14 Aug 1837 in Fermanagh, Ireland,[94] died on 13 Nov 1904,[70] and was buried in Saint John's Anglican Church Cemetery, Port Hope, Northumberland, Ontario, Canada.

     Thomas married **Margaret Ann Craig** (b. 13 Jul 1841, d. 12 Dec 1919) on 25 Dec 1861 in Northumberland, Ontario, Canada.[94]

+ 49 M   ii. **Andrew Kerr** was born about 8 May 1838 in Fermanagh, Ireland[95] and died on 8 Jun 1910 in Cobourg, Northumberland, Ontario, Canada.[14]

     Andrew married **Jane Allingham** (b. circa 1839, d. 10 Feb 1884) on 23 Jun 1859 in Saint Ninnidhs Church, Binmore Glebe, Fermanagh, Ireland.[96]

     Andrew next married **Ann Jane Coomb** (b. 1851) on 13 Nov 1884 in Port Hope, Durham, Ontario, Canada.[97]

Line of Descent from Great-Grandfather George Kerr

Line of Descent from Great-Grandfather George Kerr

Second Generation (Children)

48. Thomas Kerr[28] *(George [1])* was born on 14 Aug 1837 in Fermanagh, Ireland,[94] died on 13 Nov 1904,[70] and was buried in Saint John's Anglican Church Cemetery, Port Hope, Northumberland, Ontario, Canada.

> Birth Notes: In the 1861 census his birth year is recorded as 1837, but later his birth year was given as early as 1830.

> General Notes: He was a dairyman.

Noted events in his life were:
• Emigration: 1860, Ireland.

Thomas married **Margaret Ann Craig,** daughter of **Alexander Craig**[94] and **Elizabeth,**[94] on 25 Dec 1861 in Northumberland, Ontario, Canada.[94] Margaret Ann was born on 13 Jul 1841 in Fermanagh, Ireland[98] and died on 12 Dec 1919 in Port Hope, Northumberland, Ontario, Canada.[70]

> Research Notes: Her birth year changed between censuses. Her marriage license syas her birth year is 1841.

Children from this marriage were:

50 F   i.   **Jane Kerr** was born on 16 Jul 1863 in Ontario, Canada,[28] died on 8 Jun 1882,[70] and was buried in Port Hope, Northumberland, Ontario, Canada.[70]

51 F   ii.   **Elizabeth Kerr** was born in 1865 in Ontario, Canada.[19]

52 M   iii.   **Robert Kerr** was born in 1867 in Ontario, Canada.[26]

53 M   iv.   **Pvt. George Kerr** was born on 16 Feb 1868 in Hamilton Township, Northumberland, Ontario, Canada,[99] died on 19 Nov 1916 in Courcelette, Somme, France,[70] and was buried in Canadian National Vimy Memorial, Pas de Calais, France.

> General Notes: Served overseas in WWI. He was in the 50th Bn. of the Canadian Infantry (Alberta Regiment). His service number was 219353. Killed in action in France.

54 M   v.   **Thomas Kerr** was born in 1869.[70]

55 M   vi.   **Pvt. Thomas Kerr** was born on 26 Sep 1870 in Port Hope, Northumberland, Ontario, Canada,[70] died on 26 May 1916 in Durham, Ontario, Canada,[100] and was buried in Port Hope Union Cemetery, Port Hope, Northumberland, Ontario, Canada.[70]

> General Notes: A carpenter. His was in the 136th Battalion of the Canadian Expeditionary Force. His service number was 805092. His battalion sailed for Europe in October 1916, but he died in May 1916 of poisoning.

56 M   vii.   **Alexander Kerr** was born on 17 May 1872 in Ontario, Canada.[28]

57 M   viii.   **Andrew Kerr** was born on 24 May 1874 in Ontario, Canada.[28]

Line of Descent from Great-Grandfather George Kerr

58 M   ix. **John Kerr**[28] was born on 8 Feb 1876 in Ontario, Canada.

59 M   x. **Henry Kerr** was born in Aug 1878,[70] died on 17 Apr 1881,[70] and was buried in Port Hope, Northumberland, Ontario, Canada.[70]

49. Andrew Kerr *(George [1])* was born about 8 May 1838 in Fermanagh, Ireland[95] and died on 8 Jun 1910 in Cobourg, Northumberland, Ontario, Canada.[14]

Noted events in his life were:
- Religion: Church Of Ireland (Methodist).

- Famine: 1845-1851, Fermanagh, Ireland. During the famine the area suffered a 31% drop in population.

- Occupation: laborer, 1859, Derrygonnelly, Fermanagh, Ireland.

- Immigration: on the steamship Jura, 1 Apr 1862, Portland and Falmouth, Maine.[28] via Londonderry, Ireland leaving March 20, stopping in Maine on March 31, on his way to Ontario.

- Occupation: farmer, 1881, Hamilton Township, Northumberland, Ontario, Canada.[26]

- Occupation: farmer, 1891, Hamilton Township, Northumberland, Ontario, Canada.[27]

- Resided: 1901, Port Hope, Durham, Ontario, Canada.[101]

Andrew married **Jane Allingham,** daughter of **John Allingham,** on 23 Jun 1859 in Saint Ninnidhs Church, Binmore Glebe, Fermanagh, Ireland.[96] Jane was born circa 1839 in Ireland[102] and died on 10 Feb 1884 in Hamilton Township, Northumberland, Ontario, Canada.[14]

Marriage Notes:
"Andrew Kerr of full age, bachelor and labourer of Derrygonnelly, son of George Kerr, labourer, married Jane Allingham of full age, spinster of Drumdoonian, daughter of John Allingham, labourer, on 23 June 1859." The bride and groom signed the certificate with Xs.

Birth Notes: Jane's recorded birth year ranges from 1838 to 1841.

Noted events in her life were:
- Resided: 1859, Fermanagh, Ireland.[103] A witness at her wedding, Alex Acheson, also lived in Drumadoonia. The other witness was Richard Firth from Drummenagh Beg near Churchhill. Drumadoonia may be misspelled since it is not listed among the townlands in Fermanagh.

- Immigration: on the steamship Jura, 1 Apr 1862, Portland and Falmouth, Maine.[28] via Londonderry, Ireland leaving March 20, stopping in Maine on March 31, on her way to Ontario.

- Resided: 1871, Hamilton Township, Northumberland, Ontario, Canada.[104]

- Resided: 1881, Hamilton Township, Northumberland, Ontario, Canada.[26]

Line of Descent from Great-Grandfather George Kerr

Children from this marriage were:

60 F   i. **Margaret Jane "Jennie" Kerr** was born on 13 Feb 1861 in Derrygonnelly, Fermanagh, Ireland[105] and died on 20 Aug 1937 in Millcreek, Erie, Pennsylvania.[106]

Jennie Kerr

Noted events in her life were:

• Occupation: dressmaker, 1881, Hamilton Township, Northumberland, Ontario, Canada.[26]

• Resided: lodger and dressmaker, 1891, Cobourg, Northumberland, Ontario, Canada.[27] living with sisters Lottie and Nellie.

• Immigrated: to the USA, 1895.[107]

• Resided: with husband, 1930, Erie, Erie, Pennsylvania.[107]

Margaret Jane "Jennie" married **Joseph Frank Talling** on 6 Aug 1894 in Corry, Erie, Pennsylvania.[52] Joseph Frank was born on 11 Jul 1871 in Fenella, Ontario, Canada[108] and died on 12 Jan 1948 in Erie, Erie, Pennsylvania.[108]

Joseph Talling

Noted events in his life were:

• Immigrated: to the USA, 1889.[107]

• Occupation: car repairman, 1893, Erie, Erie, Pennsylvania.[109]

• Resided: engineer at the coal docks, 1930, Erie, Erie, Pennsylvania.[107]

• Occupation: machine operator, 1931, Erie, Erie, Pennsylvania.[54]

61 F   ii.   **Mary Ann Kerr** was born circa 1863 in Ontario, Canada.[110]

Mary Ann Kerr

Noted events in her life were:
- Resided: 1871, Hamilton Township, Northumberland, Ontario, Canada.[104]

- Occupation: tailoress, 1881, Hamilton Township, Northumberland, Ontario, Canada.[26]

- Resided: 1891, Carrick, Bruce, Ontario, Canada.[27]

Mary Ann married **George Fredrick McCullogh** on 1 Jan 1889 in Northumberland, Ontario, Canada.[111] George Fredrick was born circa 1859 in Ontario, Canada.[26]

62 M   iii.   **William George Kerr** was born on 22 Aug 1868 in Clarke, Ontario, Canada[112] and died on 5 Nov 1926 in Cobourg, Northumberland, Ontario, Canada.[14]

Noted events in his life were:
- Occupation: railroad employee.[14]

- Occupation: farmer, 1881, Hamilton Township, Northumberland, Ontario, Canada.[26]

William George married **Rose Maud "Birdie" Gibbs,** daughter of **George Gibbs**[111] and **Jane Hales,**[111] on 28 Mar 1901 in Northumberland, Ontario, Canada.[111] Rose Maud "Birdie" was born on 21 Dec 1878 in Port Hope, Ontario, Canada.[113]

Birdie Gibbs

Line of Descent from Great-Grandfather George Kerr

63 F iv. **Elinor "Nellie" Kerr** was born on 19 Mar 1870 in Baltimore, Hamilton, Northumberland, Ontario, Canada,[62] died on 30 May 1918 in Conneaut, Ashtabula, Ohio,[63] and was buried on 2 Jun 1918 in Glenwood Cemetery, Conneaut, Ashtabula, Ohio.[46]

Nellie Kerr

General Notes: Nellie Kerr's parents and eldest sister were born in Ireland and Nellie was born in Canada. She moved with two sisters, Jennie and Lottie, from their farm in Hamilton Township, Ontario, to nearby Cobourg where she worked as a dressmaker. Nellie married F.H. Heasman in Erie County, Pennsylvania and settled in Conneaut, Ohio. They had two children.

Noted events in her life were:
- Resided: 1881, Hamilton Township, Northumberland, Ontario, Canada.[26]

- Religion: Methodist, 1891.[27]

- Resided: lodger, 1891, Cobourg, Northumberland, Ontario, Canada.[27]

- Resided: 1894, Erie, Erie, Pennsylvania.[52]

- Resided: 1900, Conneaut, Ashtabula, Ohio.[53]

- Resided: at 452 State St., 1910, Conneaut, Ashtabula, Ohio.[55]

Elinor "Nellie" married **Frederick Huston "F. H." Heasman**,[46] son of **Thomas Heasman** and **Emily "Emma" Stubbs,** on 7 Aug 1894 in Corry, Erie, Pennsylvania.[52] Frederick Huston "F. H." was born on 29 Oct 1869 in New Alresford, Hampshire, England,[47] died on 6 May 1952 in Conneaut, Ashtabula, Ohio,[46] and was buried in Glenwood Cemetery, Conneaut, Ashtabula, Ohio.

F.H. Heasman

Marriage Notes: She and her sister Jennie were married one day apart in Corry, Erie, Pennsylvania.

General Notes: F.H. Heasman was born in England, immigrated with his family to Canada at the age of four, and immigrated to America at the age of twenty-five. He raised his family in Conneaut, Ohio, where he became a noted merchant and entrepreneur best known for his property called the Heasman Block and for Heasman's Grocery. He married twice: first to Nellie Kerr with whom he had his children Keith and Darrell, and second to Gertrude Zundel.[48]

Noted events in his life were:
- Immigration: 1873, Canada.[49]

- Occupation: woolen weaver, 1891, Cobourg, Northumberland, Ontario, Canada.[27]

- Occupation: railroad worker, barge worker, tugboat worker, before 1894, Canada.[50]

- Immigration: 1894, Pennsylvania.[51]

Line of Descent from Great-Grandfather George Kerr

- Resided: 1894, Harris, Ontario, Canada.[52]

- Occupation: merchant, 1900, Conneaut, Ashtabula, Ohio.[53] Residing with his wife Nellie, his brother William, and his child Keith.

- Resided: at 420 Buffalo Street, 1908, Conneaut, Ashtabula, Ohio.[54]

- Occupation: store owner, 1910, Conneaut, Ashtabula, Ohio.[55] He was a partner in Union Mercantile Company. He lived at 452 State St.

- Resided: at 378 1/2 Main Street, 1912, Conneaut, Ashtabula, Ohio.[54]

- Occupation: owner, Heasman Grocery, 382-394 Main St., 1916, Conneaut, Ashtabula, Ohio.[56]

- Resided: Heasman Block (former Baldwin Block), 1916, Conneaut, Ashtabula, Ohio.[56] In 1911, F.H. bought a grand, multi-story building on the northeast corner of Main and Mill Street -- formerly the Baldwin Block -- where he opened a dry goods store and a grocery store.

- Article: marriage notice in Conneaut News-Herald, 16 Sep 1919, Conneaut, Ashtabula, Ohio.[57]

Miss Zundel Weds Mr. F.H. Heasman

A very quiet wedding which took their many friends completely by surprise, occurred last Saturday evening when Miss Gertrude E. Zundel, daughter of Mrs. Emma Zundel, 149 Evergreen street, was united in marriage to Mr. Fred H. Heasman, well known Conneaut business man.

The wedding took place at the parsonage of the First Methodist church of this city, Rev. J. H. Blackburn, pastor of the church, conducting the ceremony which was a very simple one, the bride and groom having no attendants.

Mr. and Mrs. Heasman, accompanied by Darrell Heasman, left Saturday night for a ten days' motor trip to Canada. Upon their return they will be at home in the Heasman block, Main street.

The newly-married couple are both well known here and have many friends who will wish to extend their heartiest congratulations. Mrs. Heasman is especially well known because of her exceptional musical ability, while Mr. Heasman has been one of Conneaut's most active business men.

- Occupation: grocery store owner, 1920, Conneaut, Ashtabula, Ohio.[58]

- Bio: From History of Ashtabula County, 1924.[42]

Fred H. Heasman, a progressive and enterprising business man of Conneaut, was born in England, Oct. 29, 1869, and is a son of Thomas and Anna (Stubbs) Heasman.

The Heasman family came to Canada from England in 1872, locating at Kingston, where Thomas Heasman engaged in railroad building. He is now deceased. His wife lives at Toronto, Canada, and is 82 years of age. There were six children in the Heasman family: Frank lives in Toronto, Can.; Fred H., the subject of this sketch; Fannie married David Reid, lives in Toronto, Can.; William, lives at Moose Jaw, Saskatchewan; Alberta, married J. S. Andrews, lives in Los Angeles, Calif.; and Ernest lives in Canada. He served throughout the World War with the Canadian forces and has since been an invalid.

Fred H. Heasman was reared and educated in Canada, coming to the United States when 19 years of age, locating first in Erie, Pa. In 1896 he went to West Springfield, Pa., and engaged in the general merchandise business with W. G. Walker, under the firm name

Line of Descent from Great-Grandfather George Kerr

Walker and Heasman. In 1898 Mr. Heasman came to Conneaut and engaged in his present business. He has been located in his present building, 382-394 Main Street, since 1911. He is a general merchant and has an extensive business.

Mr. Heasman was married the first time to Miss Nellie Kerr, who died in 1918. To this union two children were born: Frederick Keith, and Darrell, who are both in business with their father. Frederick Keith Heasman was married to Miss Marion Rodgers, a native of Conneaut. Two and one-half years after the death of his first wife, Fred H. Heasman was married to Miss Gertrude Zundel, a native of Pittsburgh, Pa.

Mr. Heasman is a Republican and a member of the Rotary Club. He and his family are members of the Methodist Church, and are held in high esteem in their community.

- Occupation: manager of general store, The Heasman Co., 380-386 Main (Heasmans Block), 1930, Conneaut, Ashtabula, Ohio.[59]

- Resided: 378 Main, 1940, Conneaut, Ashtabula, Ohio.[60]

- Bio: Ashtabula County History, Then and Now, 1985.[61]

Fred H. Heasman was born in Alsford Hans [Alresford, Hants], England. He came over in a sailing boat, a six week trip and landed in Quebec, Canada, and from there to Kingston. His father was building the Great Trunk Railroad from Canada to Erie, Penn. He lived in Canada 47 years.

Fred H. Heasman sailed two years on what was a river tug.... The tug towed to Lake Huron, Sault St. Marie.... He was 19 years of age. In 1895 he came to the United States and worked in the Boston Store in Erie, Penn.

Times were hard and when 11 years old he worked in a small grocery in Michigan. Fred worked for Rushbrook Tug, Wales, towing lumber barges to Tonawanda and Black Rock, NY, Oswego, St. Clair River. He then worked for The Eaton Company, Toronto, Can., then worked for a grocer in North Bay, Ontario, married and lived two years in Canada. He then came to the United States and opened a grocery store in West Springfield, Penn, and then in Conneaut, Ohio where he was in business the rest of his life. He died in 1952.

His first wife, Nellie, died and he remarried two years later to Gertrude M. Zundel, who was a friend of the family and a bookkeeper in the Heasman Grocery and Meat Company, 378-384 Main St. Two sons were born who carried on the business having learned the business from youth. Frederick Keith learned to be manager of the grocery department and Darrell Esmond learned to run the meat department and was a first class meat cutter and manager of the meat department.

Frederick Keith was married to Marion Rogers Heasman Gruber (now) and they had one daughter, Patricia (Eagles). She and her husband, James, have one daughter, not married, who is in a nursing career and lives in California.

Darrell Esmond Heasman married Laura Jane Hogle and has one daughter, Mary Ann, who married Joseph Loren Burns. They have three children, James Joseph, Cynthia Sue and Michael Christopher. Mary Ann and Joseph Loren have three grandchildren, Kristen, Scott, and Christine.

Mary Ann and Joseph Loren Burns live in Bellvue, Ohio. Their son, James, and family also live in Bellvue. Their daughter, Cynthia Sue, and family live in Hillsboro, Ohio. She is married to Richard D. Eigel, a meat inspector for the government. Cynthia Sue teaches music (band and choir) in the Hillsboro High School.

Frederick Keith was born in 1899 and died in 1960 (age 61). Darrell Esmond was born Feb 12, 1901 and died Sept. 18, 1954 (age 52).

Mary Ann and Joseph Loren's son, Michael C., is a junior in high school, being born the year that his older brother, James Joseph, was graduating from High School.

Line of Descent from Great-Grandfather George Kerr

Darrell and Laura built a summer home at 853 Lakeview Ave. in Conneaut, Ohio, where Laura still lives since her husband's death, to build up Social Security, as they did not have Social Security when her husband was living. The Heasman Meat and Grocery Store was torn down in July, 1962, to make room to build the Kroger Store, which is now vacant.

Marian Heasman Gruber, is widow of her second husband, Henry Gruber, who formerly owned "The Syndicate," a woman's apparel store. She is now living in Ashtabula County Nursing Home in Kingsville, Ohio.

• Bio: Patricia Heasman oral history, 2002.[48]

F.H. came to Canada from England -- six weeks on a sail boat -- and landed in Quebec, then moved to Kingston, Ontario. F.H. and his father helped build the Grand Trunk RR between Ontario and Erie. His first job was in a grocery at 11 years, at 19 years sailed on river tugs for two years towing barges to Lake Huron, and then worked at Wales, Ontario on the tug Walter Rushbrook, ferrying boats up the St. Clair River. He also worked as a lumberjack, and at Eaton Department Store in Toronto. There he met Charlie Crombie, both married and lived in Toronto for about 2 years, before coming to the States. In 1895 Fred and Nellie Heasman moved to Erie, Pennsylvania. F.H. worked in a carpet department store in Erie, Pennsylvania, called the Boston Store. He opened a grocery store in West Springfield, Pennsylvania. Charlie Crombie opened a grocery on State Street in Conneaut (across from the now Silver Diner). Fred bought the Baldwin Block on the corner of Main & Mill Streets in Conneaut and opened the Heasman Grocery and Meat Company in about 1900. His sons Frederick Keith and Darrel Esmond both worked there.

----

64 F   v. **Charlotte Elizabeth "Lottie" Kerr** was born circa 1880 in Ontario, Canada.[26]

Noted events in her life were:
• Resided: lodger, Cobourg, Northumberland, Ontario, Canada.[27] with Jennie and Nellie.

Lottie Kerr

Charlotte Elizabeth "Lottie" married **Charles Alfred Johnston** in 1911 in Middlesex, Ontario, Canada.[43]

Andrew next married **Ann Jane Coomb,** daughter of **Thomas Coomb**[111] and **Jane,**[111] on 13 Nov 1884 in Port Hope, Durham, Ontario, Canada.[97] Ann Jane was born in 1851 in Hamilton Township, Northumberland, Ontario, Canada.[114]

Line of Descent from Great-Grandfather John Allingham

First Generation

65. John Allingham was born about 1810.

> Research Notes: John Allingham is listed as a landholder in Sandhill near Derrygonnelly in Griffith Valuations. He sublet his home from Alexander Acheson and leased 65 acres from Mervyn Edward Archdale, MP.

Noted events in his life were:
* Land: 1862, Sandhill, Fermanagh, Ireland.[115]

John married someone.

His child was:

+ 66 F   i. **Jane Allingham** was born circa 1839 in Ireland[102] and died on 10 Feb 1884 in Hamilton Township, Northumberland, Ontario, Canada.[14]

Jane married **Andrew Kerr** (b. about 8 May 1838, d. 8 Jun 1910) on 23 Jun 1859 in Saint Ninnidhs Church, Binmore Glebe, Fermanagh, Ireland.[96]

(Duplicate Line. See Person 49)

Line of Descent from Great-Grandfather John Allingham

Line of Descent from Great-Grandfather John Allingham

Second Generation (Children)

66. Jane Allingham *(John¹)* was born circa 1839 in Ireland[102] and died on 10 Feb 1884 in Hamilton Township, Northumberland, Ontario, Canada.[14]

> Birth Notes: Jane's recorded birth year ranges from 1838 to 1841.

Noted events in her life were:
- Resided: 1859, Fermanagh, Ireland.[103] A witness at her wedding, Alex Acheson, also lived in Drumadoonia. The other witness was Richard Firth from Drummenagh Beg near Churchhill. Drumadoonia may be misspelled since it is not listed among the townlands in Fermanagh.
- Immigration: on the steamship Jura, 1 Apr 1862, Portland and Falmouth, Maine.[28] via Londonderry, Ireland leaving March 20, stopping in Maine on March 31, on her way to Ontario.
- Resided: 1871, Hamilton Township, Northumberland, Ontario, Canada.[104]
- Resided: 1881, Hamilton Township, Northumberland, Ontario, Canada.[26]

Jane married **Andrew Kerr,** son of **George Kerr**[14] and **Jane,** on 23 Jun 1859 in Saint Ninnidhs Church, Binmore Glebe, Fermanagh, Ireland.[96] Andrew was born about 8 May 1838 in Fermanagh, Ireland[95] and died on 8 Jun 1910 in Cobourg, Northumberland, Ontario, Canada.[14]

> Marriage Notes:
> "Andrew Kerr of full age, bachelor and labourer of Derrygonnelly, son of George Kerr, labourer, married Jane Allingham of full age, spinster of Drumdoonian, daughter of John Allingham, labourer, on 23 June 1859." The bride and groom signed the certificate with Xs.

Noted events in his life were:
- Religion: Church Of Ireland (Methodist).
- Famine: 1845-1851, Fermanagh, Ireland. During the famine the area suffered a 31% drop in population.
- Occupation: laborer, 1859, Derrygonnelly, Fermanagh, Ireland.
- Immigration: on the steamship Jura, 1 Apr 1862, Portland and Falmouth, Maine.[28] via Londonderry, Ireland leaving March 20, stopping in Maine on March 31, on his way to Ontario.
- Occupation: farmer, 1881, Hamilton Township, Northumberland, Ontario, Canada.[26]
- Occupation: farmer, 1891, Hamilton Township, Northumberland, Ontario, Canada.[27]
- Resided: 1901, Port Hope, Durham, Ontario, Canada.[101]

(Duplicate Line. See Person 49)

Ancestor Chart for Frederick Keith Heasman

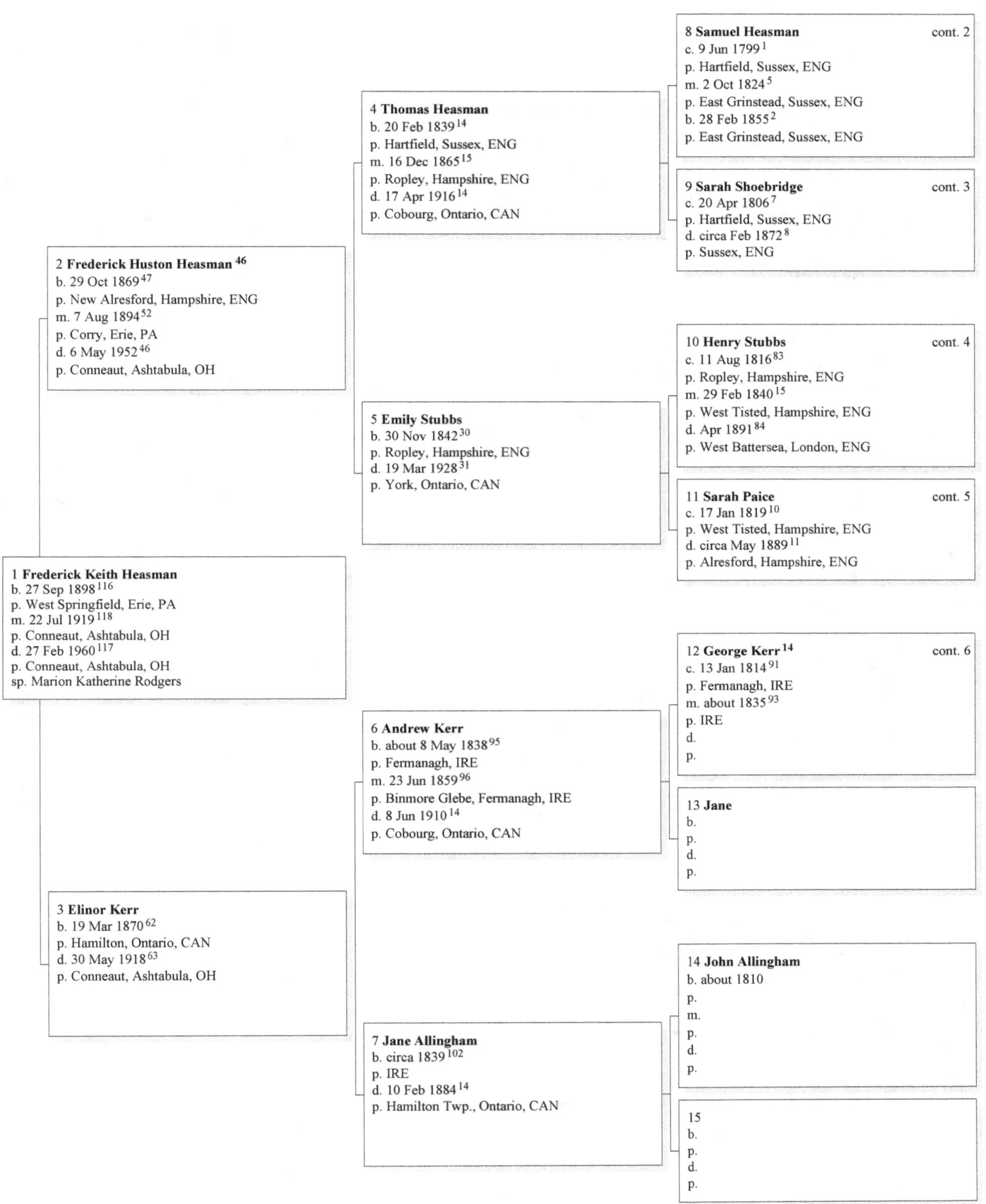

Ancestor Chart for Frederick Keith Heasman

No. 1 on this chart is the same as no. 8 on chart no. 1

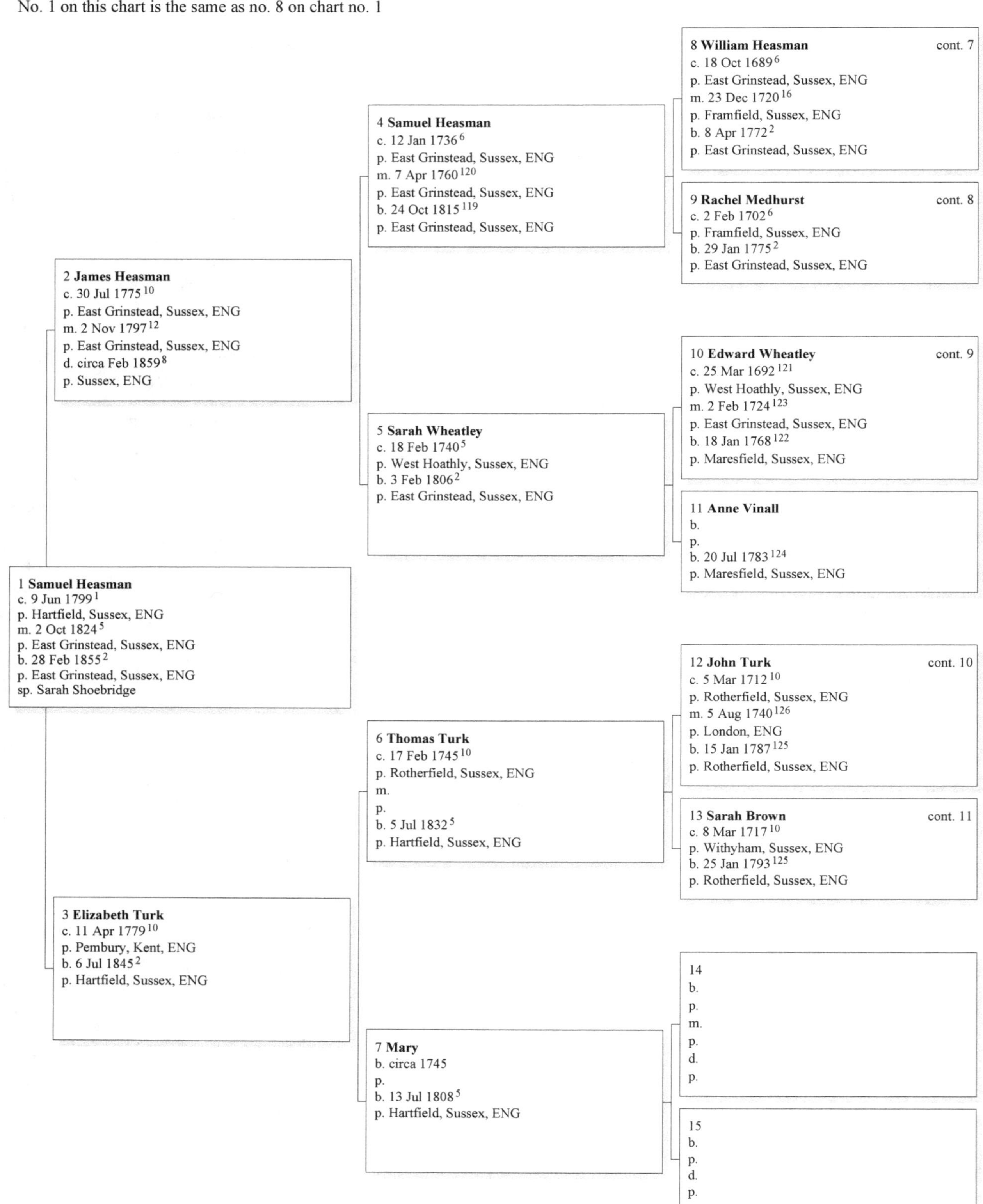

8 William Heasman   cont. 7
c. 18 Oct 1689 [6]
p. East Grinstead, Sussex, ENG
m. 23 Dec 1720 [16]
p. Framfield, Sussex, ENG
b. 8 Apr 1772 [2]
p. East Grinstead, Sussex, ENG

9 Rachel Medhurst   cont. 8
c. 2 Feb 1702 [6]
p. Framfield, Sussex, ENG
b. 29 Jan 1775 [2]
p. East Grinstead, Sussex, ENG

4 Samuel Heasman
c. 12 Jan 1736 [6]
p. East Grinstead, Sussex, ENG
m. 7 Apr 1760 [120]
p. East Grinstead, Sussex, ENG
b. 24 Oct 1815 [119]
p. East Grinstead, Sussex, ENG

10 Edward Wheatley   cont. 9
c. 25 Mar 1692 [121]
p. West Hoathly, Sussex, ENG
m. 2 Feb 1724 [123]
p. East Grinstead, Sussex, ENG
b. 18 Jan 1768 [122]
p. Maresfield, Sussex, ENG

11 Anne Vinall
b.
p.
b. 20 Jul 1783 [124]
p. Maresfield, Sussex, ENG

5 Sarah Wheatley
c. 18 Feb 1740 [5]
p. West Hoathly, Sussex, ENG
b. 3 Feb 1806 [2]
p. East Grinstead, Sussex, ENG

2 James Heasman
c. 30 Jul 1775 [10]
p. East Grinstead, Sussex, ENG
m. 2 Nov 1797 [12]
p. East Grinstead, Sussex, ENG
d. circa Feb 1859 [8]
p. Sussex, ENG

1 Samuel Heasman
c. 9 Jun 1799 [1]
p. Hartfield, Sussex, ENG
m. 2 Oct 1824 [5]
p. East Grinstead, Sussex, ENG
b. 28 Feb 1855 [2]
p. East Grinstead, Sussex, ENG
sp. Sarah Shoebridge

12 John Turk   cont. 10
c. 5 Mar 1712 [10]
p. Rotherfield, Sussex, ENG
m. 5 Aug 1740 [126]
p. London, ENG
b. 15 Jan 1787 [125]
p. Rotherfield, Sussex, ENG

13 Sarah Brown   cont. 11
c. 8 Mar 1717 [10]
p. Withyham, Sussex, ENG
b. 25 Jan 1793 [125]
p. Rotherfield, Sussex, ENG

6 Thomas Turk
c. 17 Feb 1745 [10]
p. Rotherfield, Sussex, ENG
m.
p.
b. 5 Jul 1832 [5]
p. Hartfield, Sussex, ENG

14
b.
p.
m.
p.
d.
p.

15
b.
p.
d.
p.

3 Elizabeth Turk
c. 11 Apr 1779 [10]
p. Pembury, Kent, ENG
b. 6 Jul 1845 [2]
p. Hartfield, Sussex, ENG

7 Mary
b. circa 1745
p.
b. 13 Jul 1808 [5]
p. Hartfield, Sussex, ENG

Ancestor Chart for Frederick Keith Heasman

No. 1 on this chart is the same as no. 9 on chart no. 1

8 John Shewbridge   cont. 12
c. 31 Jul 1698 [1]
p. Hartfield, Sussex, ENG
m. 19 Feb 1723 [12]
p. Hartfield, Sussex, ENG
b. 28 Dec 1770 [125]
p. Hartfield, Sussex, ENG

9 Mary Pollard   cont. 13
c. 15 Jun 1699 [1]
p. Hartfield, Sussex, ENG
d.
p.

4 John Shoebridge [7]
c. 31 Dec 1723 [10]
p. Hartfield, Sussex, ENG
m. 8 May 1760 [15]
p. Hartfield, Sussex, ENG
b. 20 Dec 1794 [125]
p. Hartfield, Sussex, ENG

10 Thomas Wood [10]   cont. 14
c. 7 Jun 1705 [10]
p. East Grinstead, Sussex, ENG
m. 4 Apr 1733 [12]
p. East Grinstead, Sussex, ENG
b. 21 Dec 1761 [5]
p. East Grinstead, Sussex, ENG

11 Ann Butching [10]   cont. 15
c. 2 Feb 1703 [10]
p. East Grinstead, Sussex, ENG
b. 22 Jan 1780 [125]
p. East Grinstead, Sussex, ENG

5 Elizabeth Wood [131]
c. 23 Mar 1739 [10]
p. East Grinstead, Sussex, ENG
b. 9 Dec 1813 [125]
p. Hartfield, Sussex, ENG

2 Jesse Shoebridge [6]
c. 21 Jul 1776 [127]
p. Hartfield, Sussex, ENG
m. 19 Mar 1803 [129]
p. Hartfield, Sussex, ENG
b. 1 Feb 1848 [2]
p. Hartfield, Sussex, ENG

1 Sarah Shoebridge
c. 20 Apr 1806 [7]
p. Hartfield, Sussex, ENG
m. 2 Oct 1824 [5]
p. East Grinstead, Sussex, ENG
d. circa Feb 1872 [8]
p. Sussex, ENG
sp. Samuel Heasman

12 George Weller [10]
c. circa 1700
p.
m.
p.
d.
p.

6 William Weller [1]
c. 31 Aug 1726 [10]
p. Speldhurst, Kent, ENG
m. 10 Oct 1751 [15]
p. Bidborough, Kent, ENG
b. 4 Apr 1777 [125]
p. Speldhurst, Kent, ENG

13 Mary [10]
b.
p.
d.
p.

3 Karen Weller
c. 19 Jun 1774 [1]
p. Ashurst, Kent, ENG
b. 5 May 1860 [130]
p. Hartfield, Sussex, ENG

14 Benjamin Andrews [10]
b.
p.
m.
p.
d.
p.

7 Sarah Andrews
c. 6 Dec 1732 [10]
p. Ashurst, Kent, ENG
b. 20 Apr 1791 [125]
p. Speldhurst, Kent, ENG

15
b.
p.
d.
p.

Ancestor Chart for Frederick Keith Heasman

No. 1 on this chart is the same as no. 10 on chart no. 1

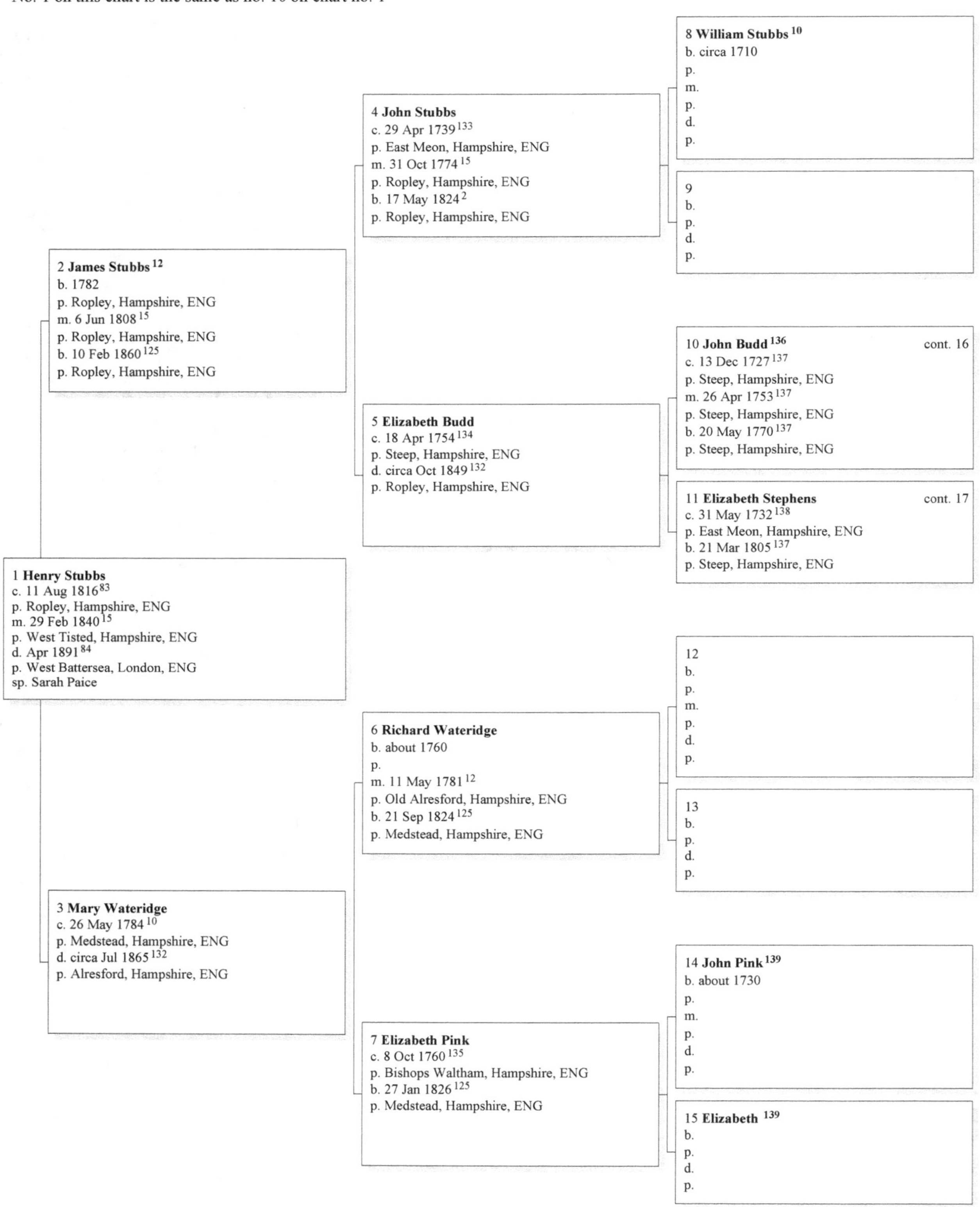

1 Henry Stubbs
c. 11 Aug 1816 [83]
p. Ropley, Hampshire, ENG
m. 29 Feb 1840 [15]
p. West Tisted, Hampshire, ENG
d. Apr 1891 [84]
p. West Battersea, London, ENG
sp. Sarah Paice

2 James Stubbs [12]
b. 1782
p. Ropley, Hampshire, ENG
m. 6 Jun 1808 [15]
p. Ropley, Hampshire, ENG
b. 10 Feb 1860 [125]
p. Ropley, Hampshire, ENG

3 Mary Wateridge
c. 26 May 1784 [10]
p. Medstead, Hampshire, ENG
d. circa Jul 1865 [132]
p. Alresford, Hampshire, ENG

4 John Stubbs
c. 29 Apr 1739 [133]
p. East Meon, Hampshire, ENG
m. 31 Oct 1774 [15]
p. Ropley, Hampshire, ENG
b. 17 May 1824 [2]
p. Ropley, Hampshire, ENG

5 Elizabeth Budd
c. 18 Apr 1754 [134]
p. Steep, Hampshire, ENG
d. circa Oct 1849 [132]
p. Ropley, Hampshire, ENG

6 Richard Wateridge
b. about 1760
p.
m. 11 May 1781 [12]
p. Old Alresford, Hampshire, ENG
b. 21 Sep 1824 [125]
p. Medstead, Hampshire, ENG

7 Elizabeth Pink
c. 8 Oct 1760 [135]
p. Bishops Waltham, Hampshire, ENG
b. 27 Jan 1826 [125]
p. Medstead, Hampshire, ENG

8 William Stubbs [10]
b. circa 1710
p.
m.
p.
d.
p.

9
b.
p.
d.
p.

10 John Budd [136]   cont. 16
c. 13 Dec 1727 [137]
p. Steep, Hampshire, ENG
m. 26 Apr 1753 [137]
p. Steep, Hampshire, ENG
b. 20 May 1770 [137]
p. Steep, Hampshire, ENG

11 Elizabeth Stephens   cont. 17
c. 31 May 1732 [138]
p. East Meon, Hampshire, ENG
b. 21 Mar 1805 [137]
p. Steep, Hampshire, ENG

12
b.
p.
m.
p.
d.
p.

13
b.
p.
d.
p.

14 John Pink [139]
b. about 1730
p.
m.
p.
d.
p.

15 Elizabeth [139]
b.
p.
d.
p.

Ancestor Chart for Frederick Keith Heasman

No. 1 on this chart is the same as no. 11 on chart no. 1

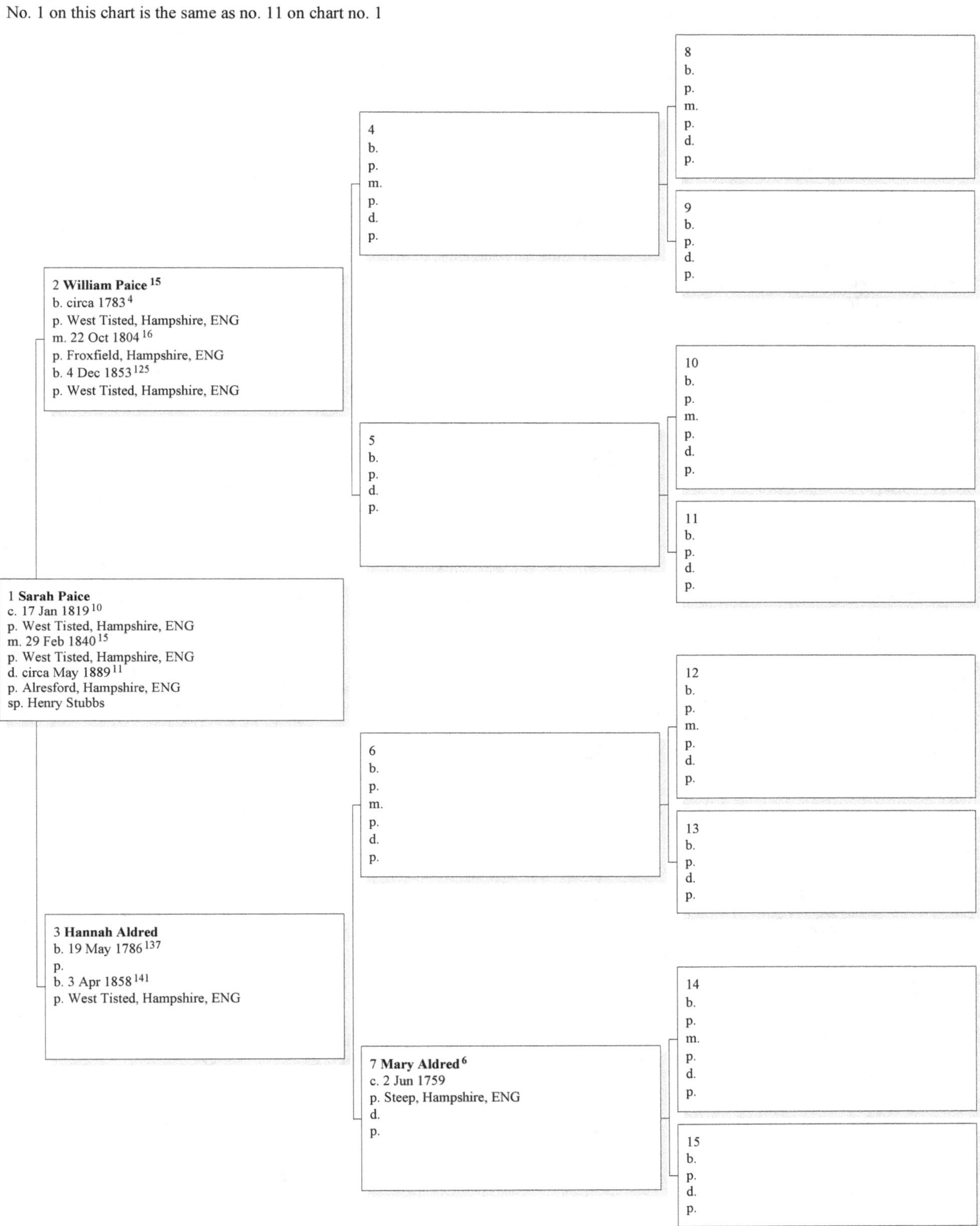

Ancestor Chart for Frederick Keith Heasman

No. 1 on this chart is the same as no. 12 on chart no. 1

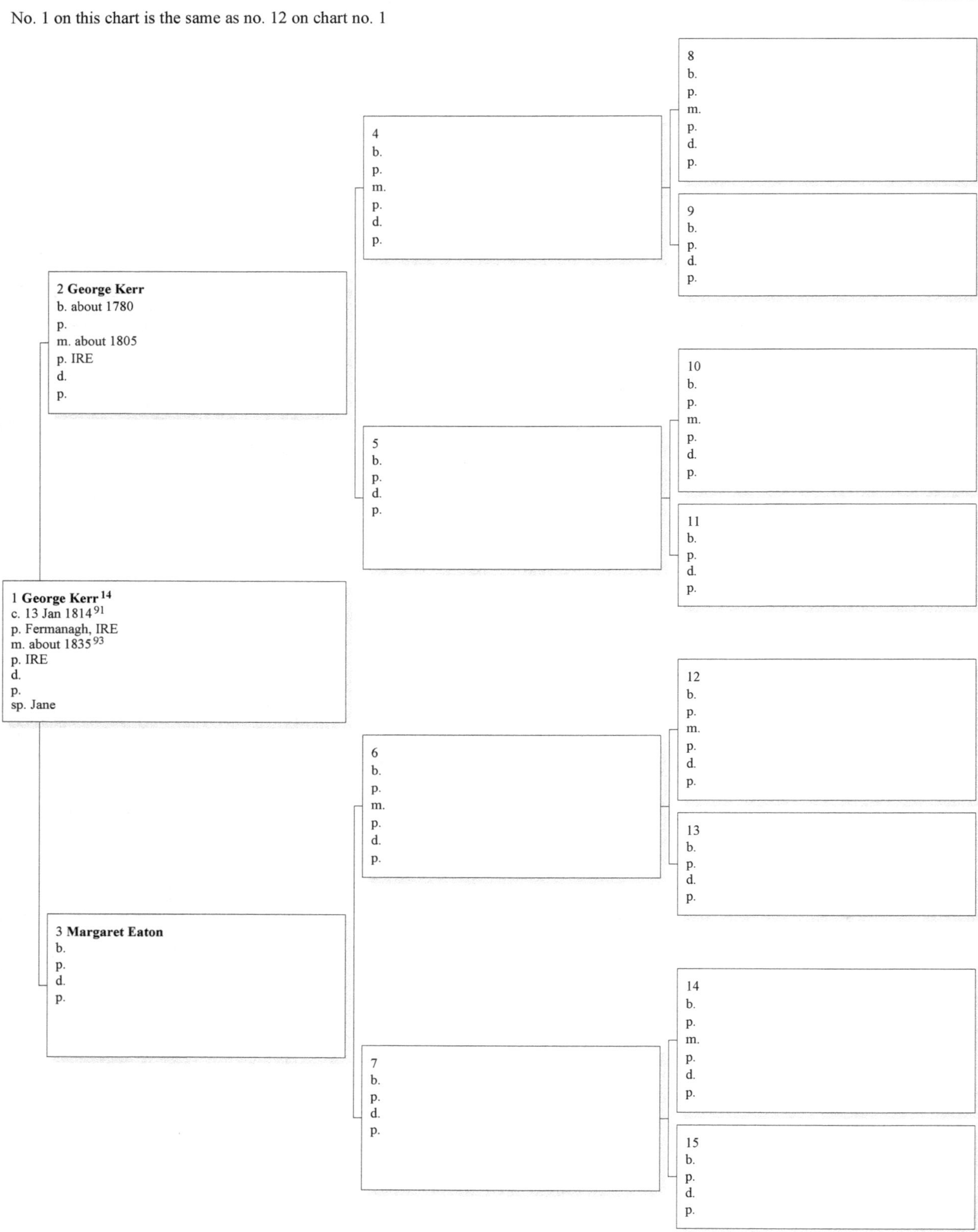

Ancestor Chart for Frederick Keith Heasman

No. 1 on this chart is the same as no. 8 on chart no. 2

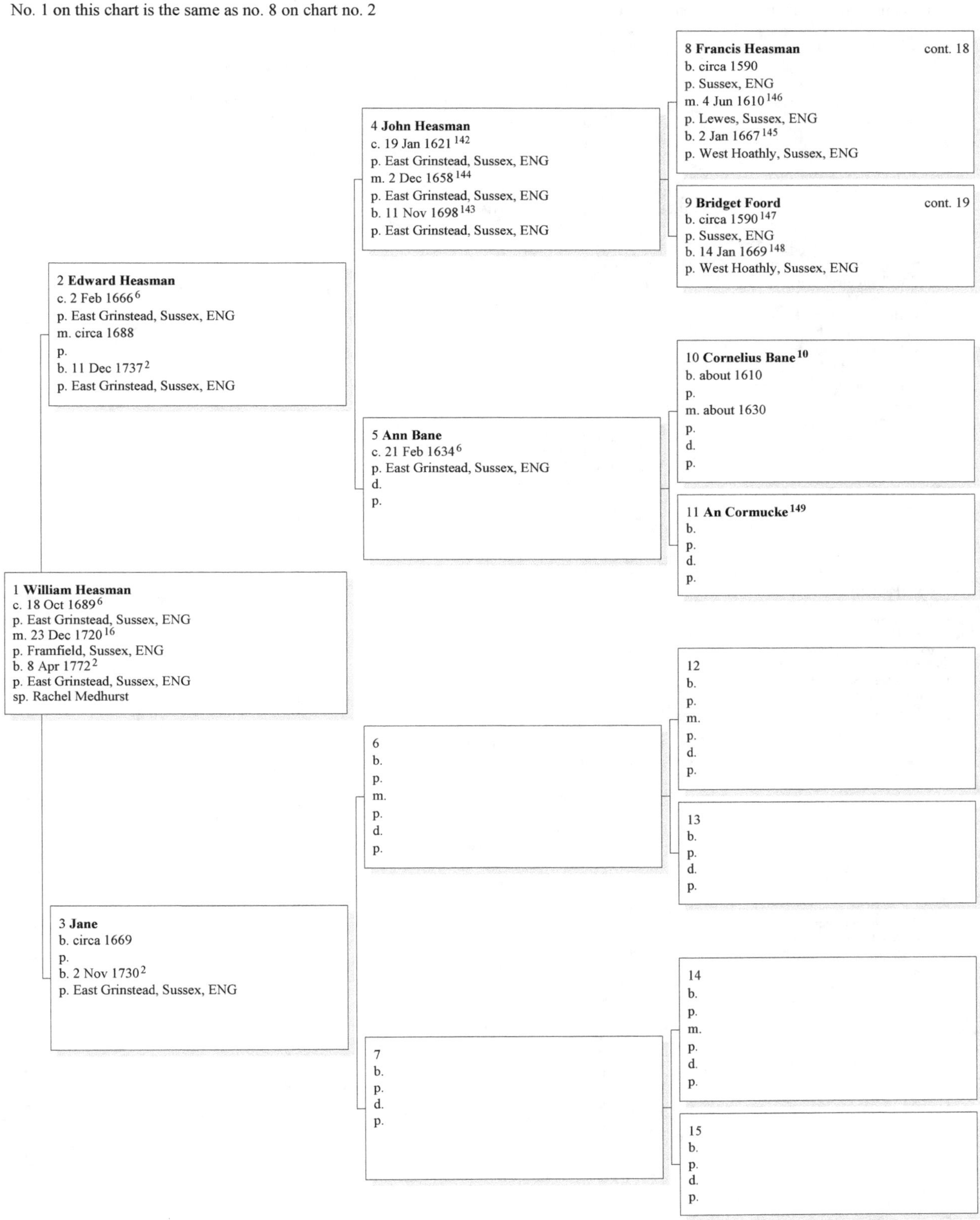

Ancestor Chart for Frederick Keith Heasman

No. 1 on this chart is the same as no. 9 on chart no. 2

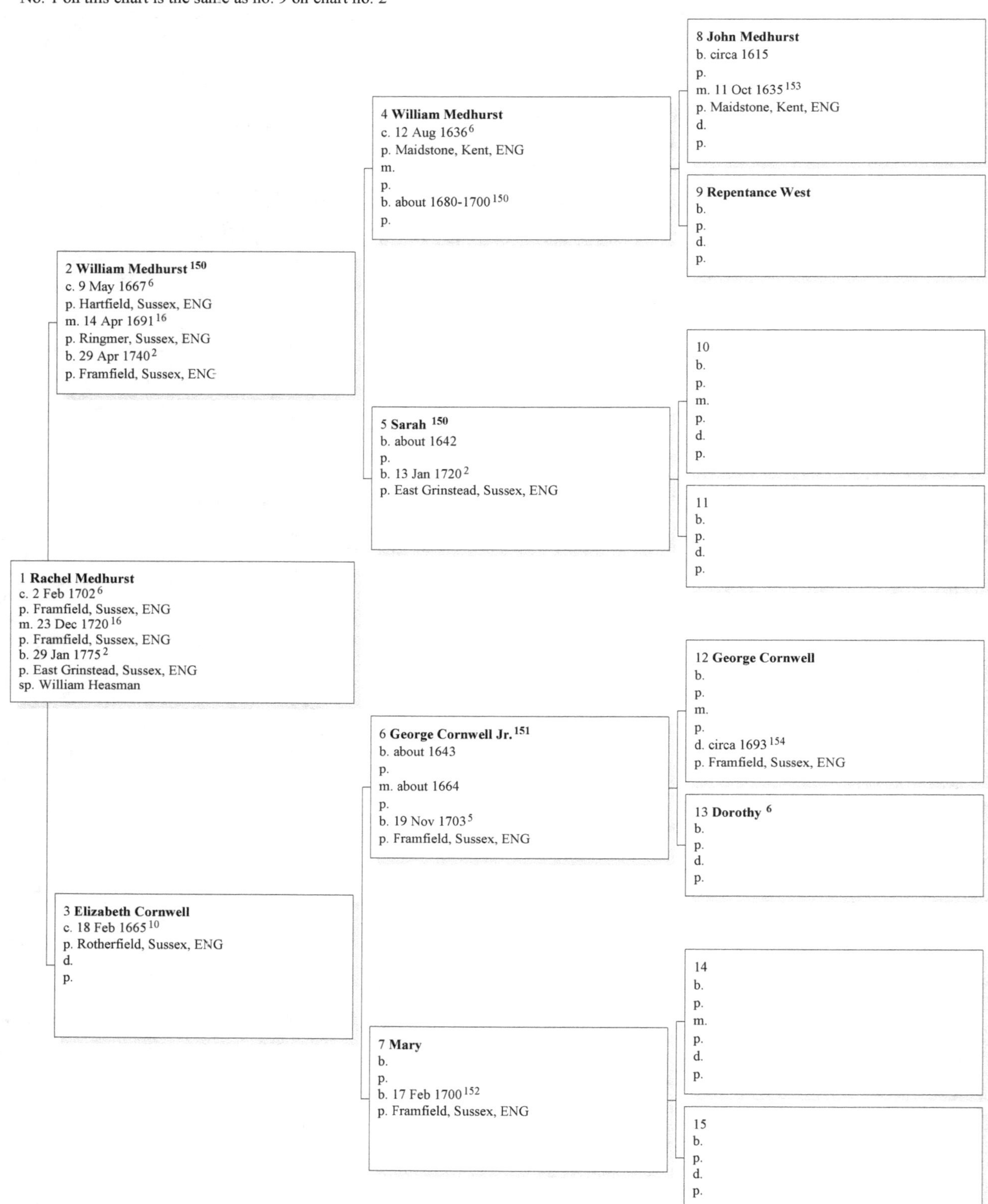

Ancestor Chart for Frederick Keith Heasman

No. 1 on this chart is the same as no. 10 on chart no. 2

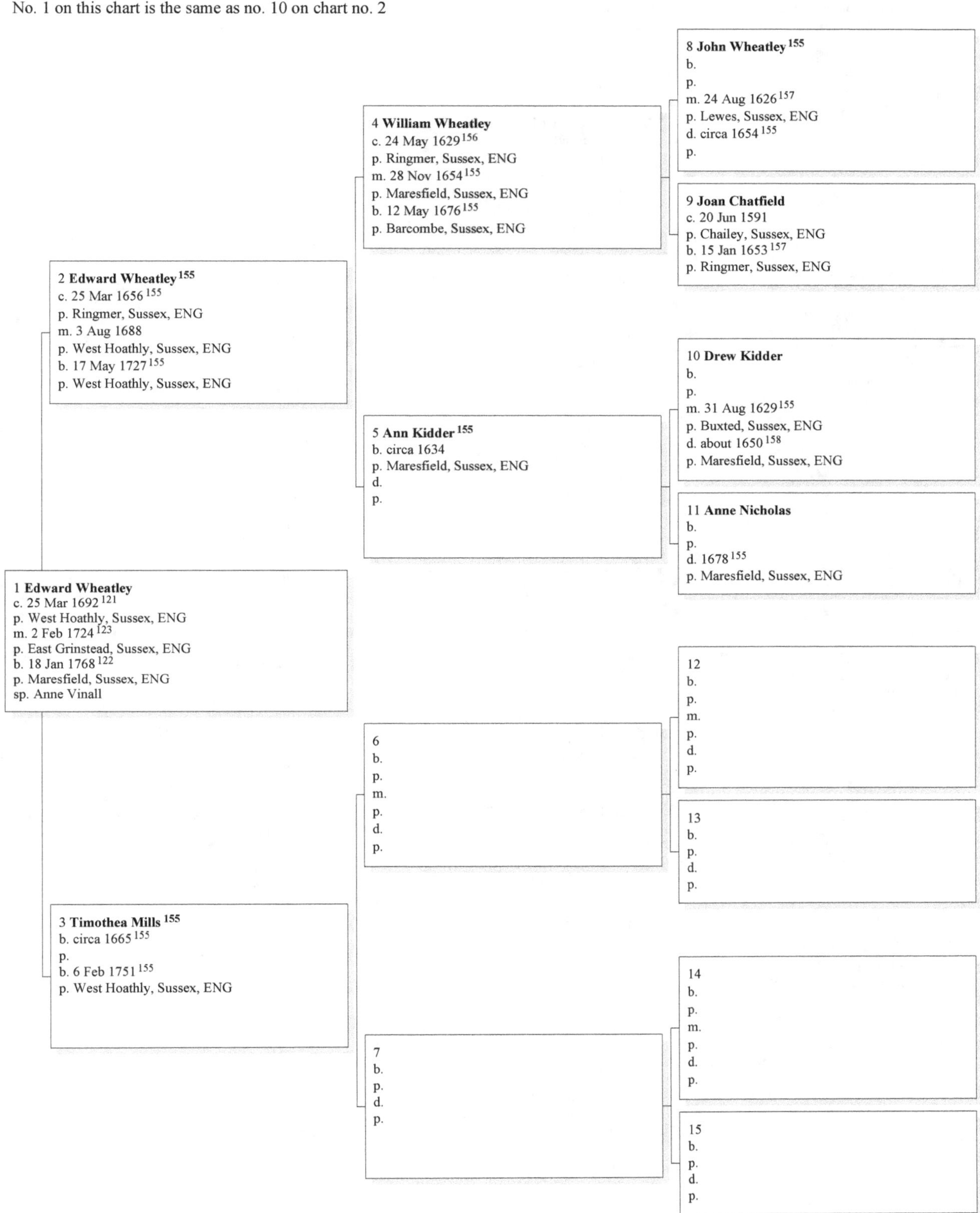

Ancestor Chart for Frederick Keith Heasman

No. 1 on this chart is the same as no. 12 on chart no. 2

8
b.
p.
m.
p.
d.
p.

4 John Turk
b. about 1655
p.
m. circa 1680
p.
b. 22 Sep 1705 [125]
p. Rotherfield, Sussex, ENG

9
b.
p.
d.
p.

2 John Turk
c. 3 Jul 1681 [10]
p. Rotherfield, Sussex, ENG
m. 23 Oct 1705 [16]
p. Lewes, Sussex, ENG
b. 5 Apr 1740 [125]
p. Rotherfield, Sussex, ENG

10
b.
p.
m.
p.
d.
p.

5 Mary
b. about 1655
p.
b. 16 Sep 1704 [125]
p. Rotherfield, Sussex, ENG

11
b.
p.
d.
p.

1 John Turk
c. 5 Mar 1712 [10]
p. Rotherfield, Sussex, ENG
m. 5 Aug 1740 [126]
p. London, ENG
b. 15 Jan 1787 [125]
p. Rotherfield, Sussex, ENG
sp. Sarah Brown

12 William Browne
b. circa 1620
p.
m. 19 Jul 1640 [161]
p. Lewes, Sussex, ENG
b. 10 Mar 1674 [160]
p. Withyham, Sussex, ENG

6 William Browne [159]
b. about 1643
p.
m. 11 May 1671 [12]
p. Withyham, Sussex, ENG
d.
p.

13 Elizabeth Groombridge   cont. 20
b. circa 1620
p.
b. 20 Feb 1684 [160]
p. Withyham, Sussex, ENG

3 Sarah Browne
c. 25 May 1675 [10]
p. Withyham, Sussex, ENG
b. 12 Feb 1758 [125]
p. Rotherfield, Sussex, ENG

14
b.
p.
m.
p.
d.
p.

7 Katherine Longly
b. about 1650
p.
b. 1 Jun 1722 [22]
p. Withyham, Sussex, ENG

15
b.
p.
d.
p.

Ancestor Chart for Frederick Keith Heasman

No. 1 on this chart is the same as no. 13 on chart no. 2

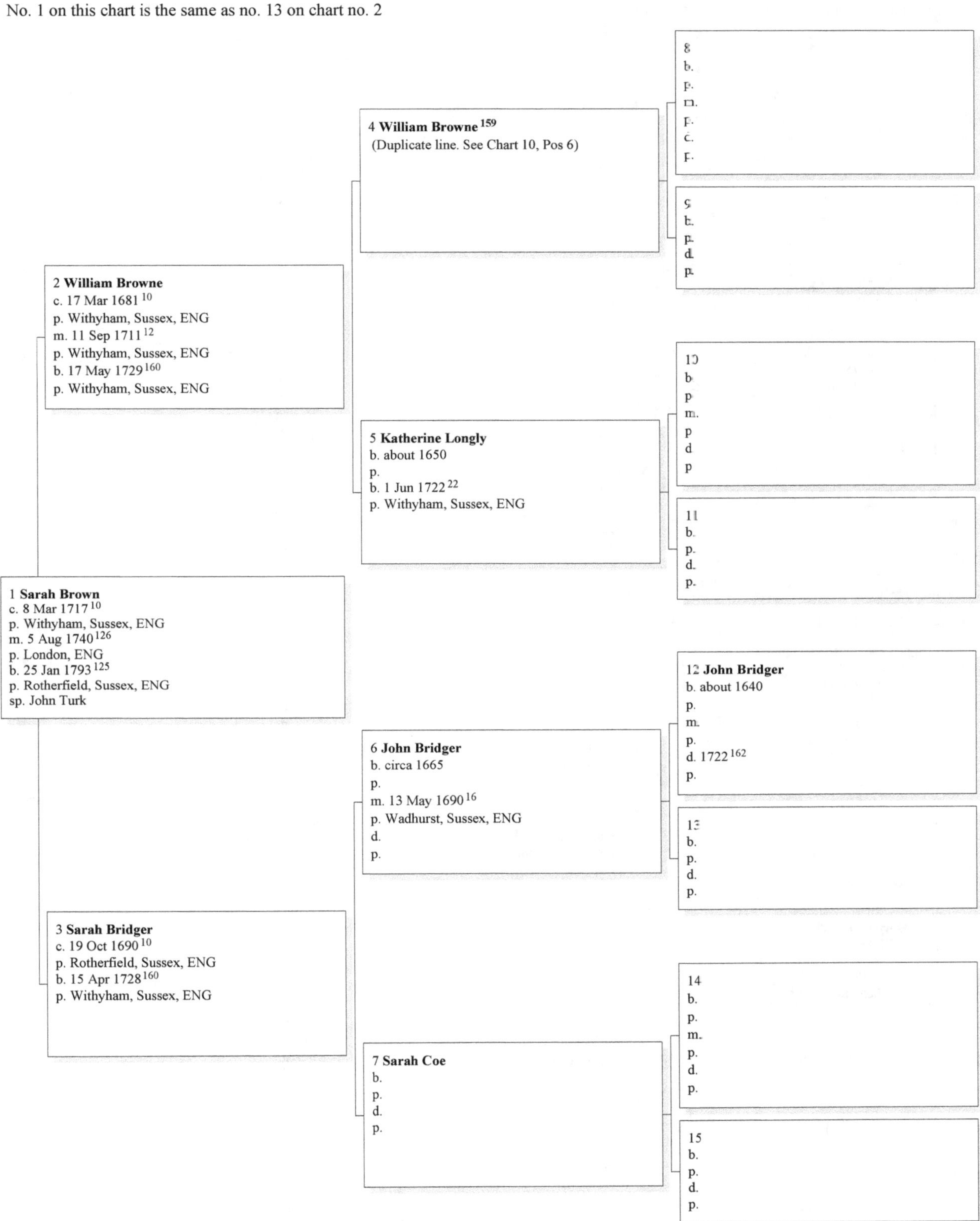

Ancestor Chart for Frederick Keith Heasman

No. 1 on this chart is the same as no. 8 on chart no. 3

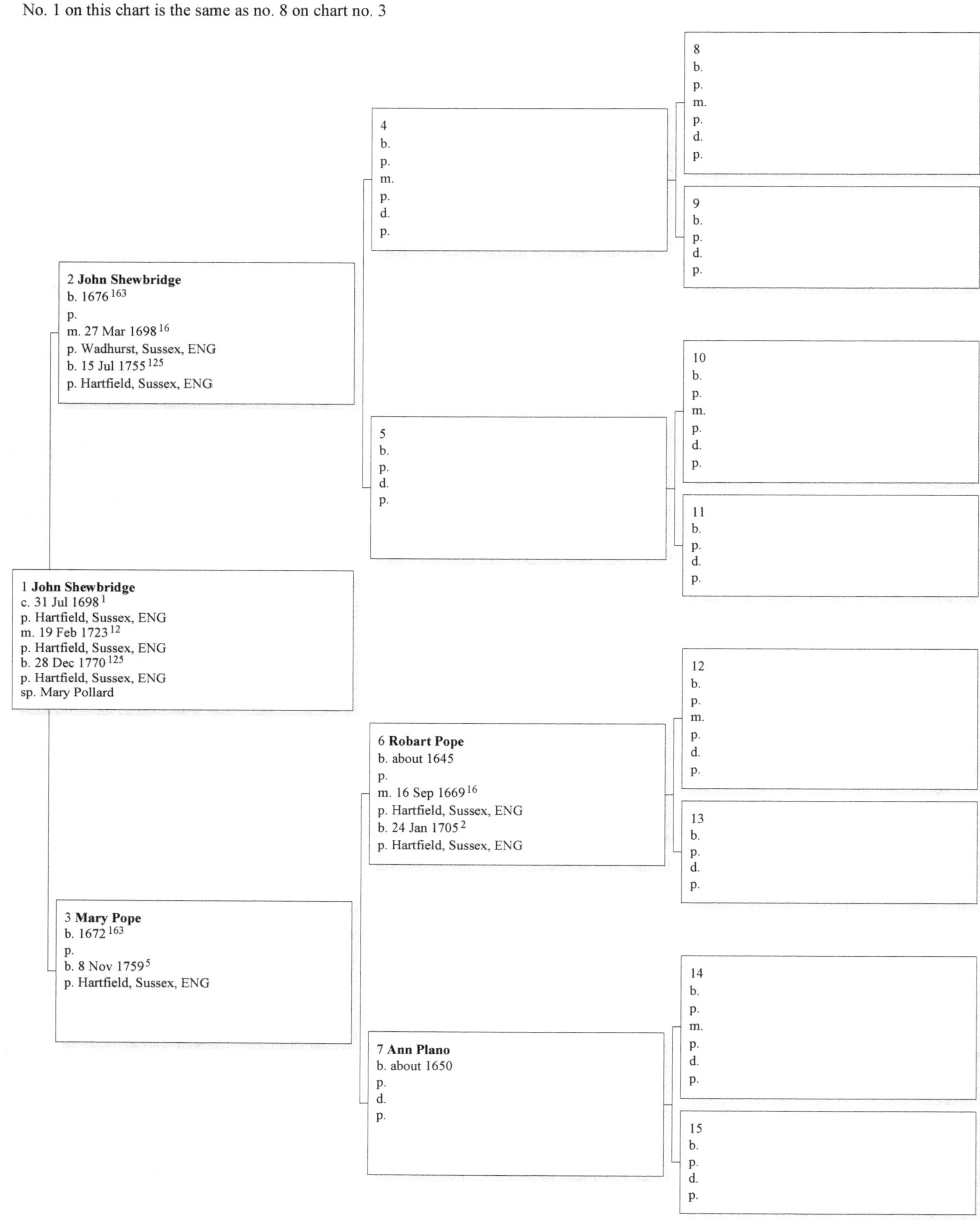

Ancestor Chart for Frederick Keith Heasman

No. 1 on this chart is the same as no. 9 on chart no. 3

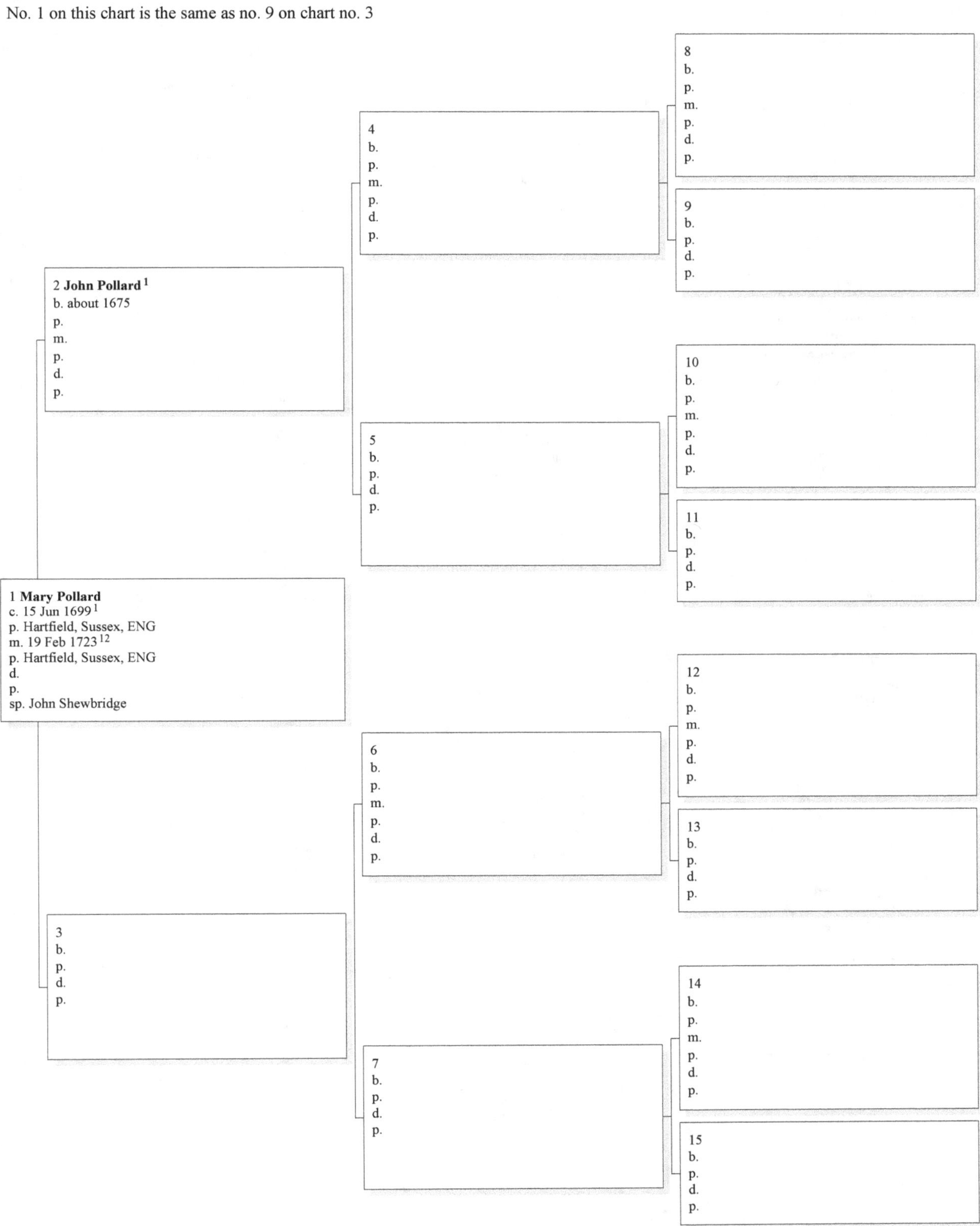

Ancestor Chart for Frederick Keith Heasman

No. 1 on this chart is the same as no. 10 on chart no. 3

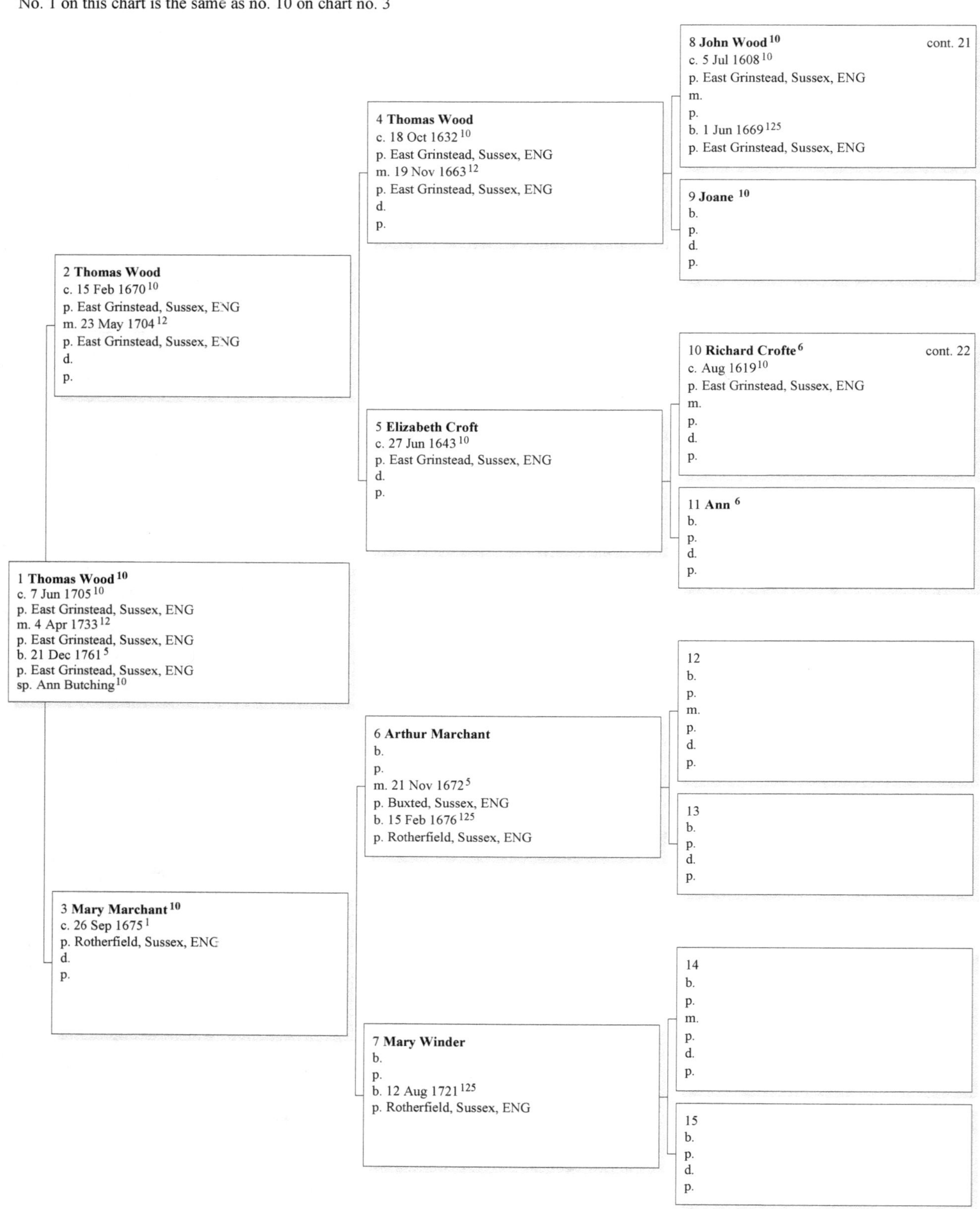

Ancestor Chart for Frederick Keith Heasman

No. 1 on this chart is the same as no. 11 on chart no. 3

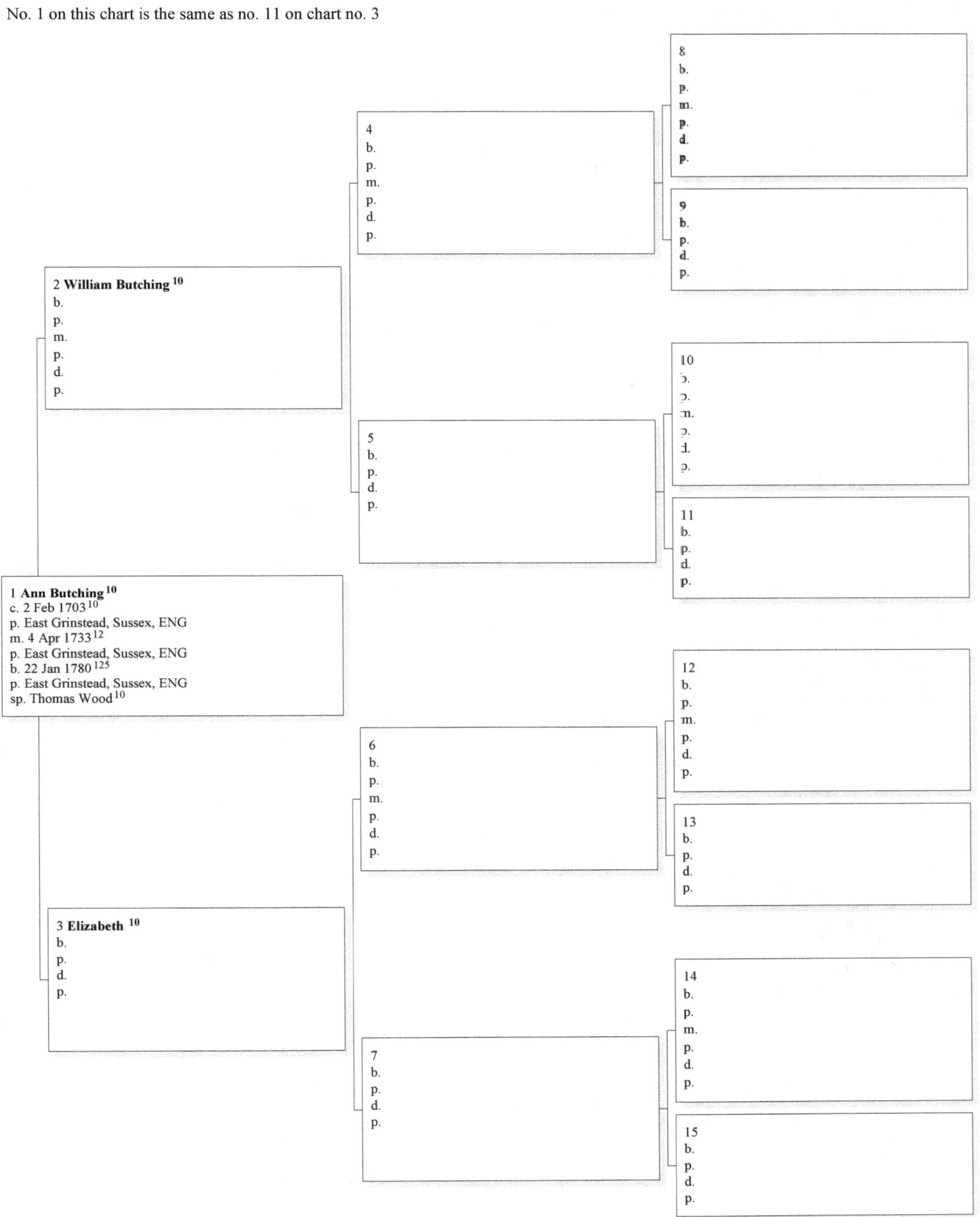

Ancestor Chart for Frederick Keith Heasman

No. 1 on this chart is the same as no. 10 on chart no. 4

Ancestor Chart for Frederick Keith Heasman

No. 1 on this chart is the same as no. 11 on chart no. 4

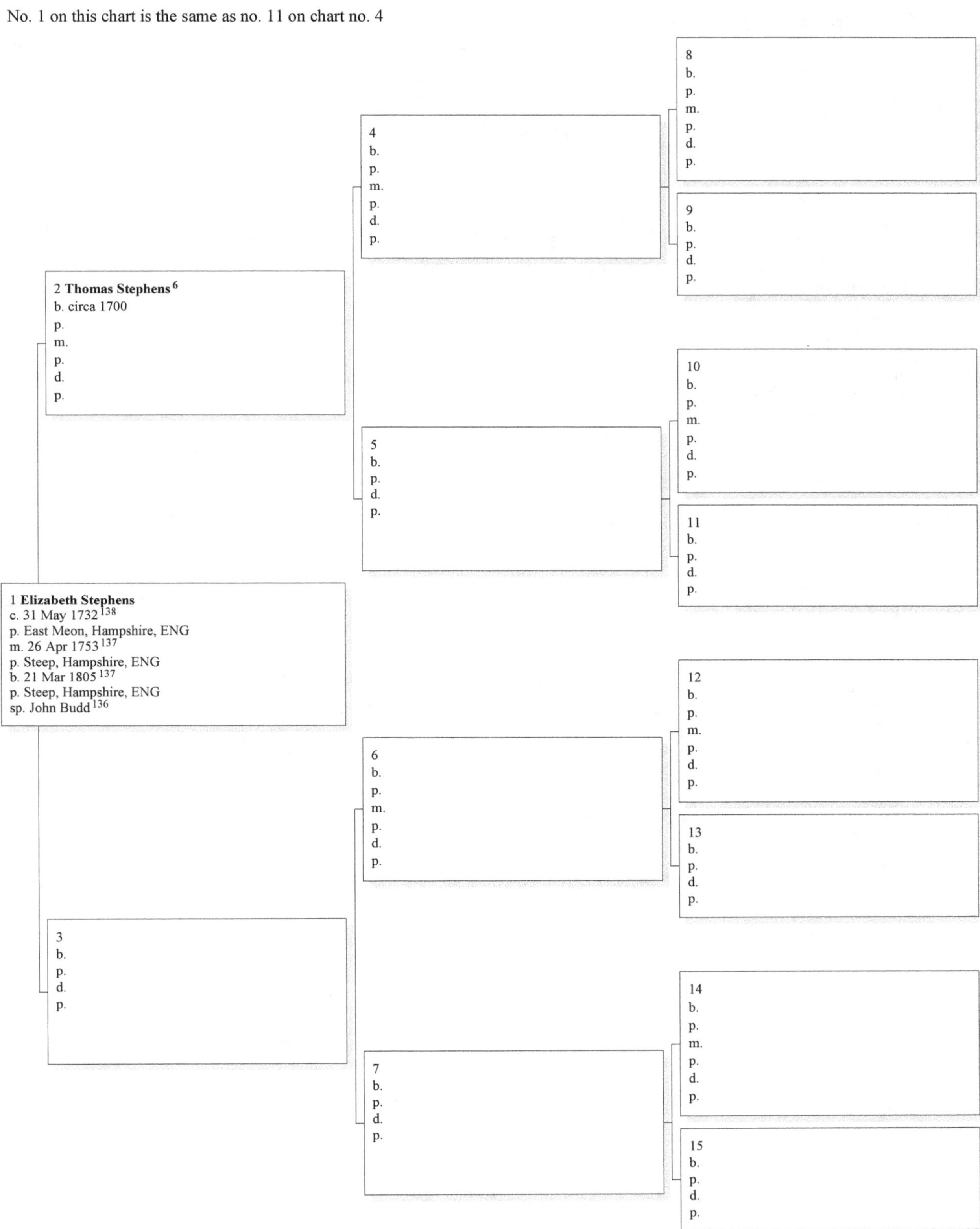

Ancestor Chart for Frederick Keith Heasman

No. 1 on this chart is the same as no. 8 on chart no. 7

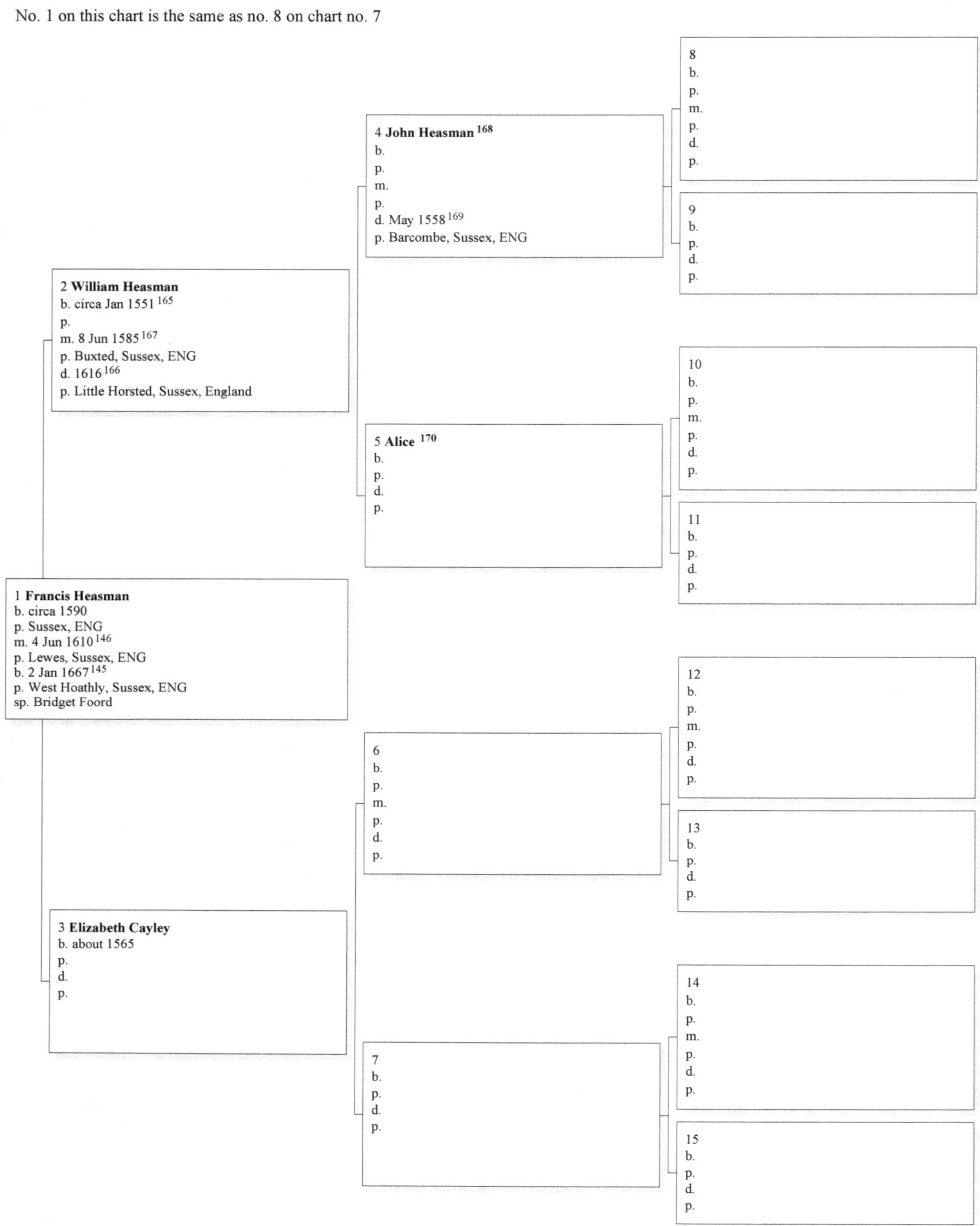

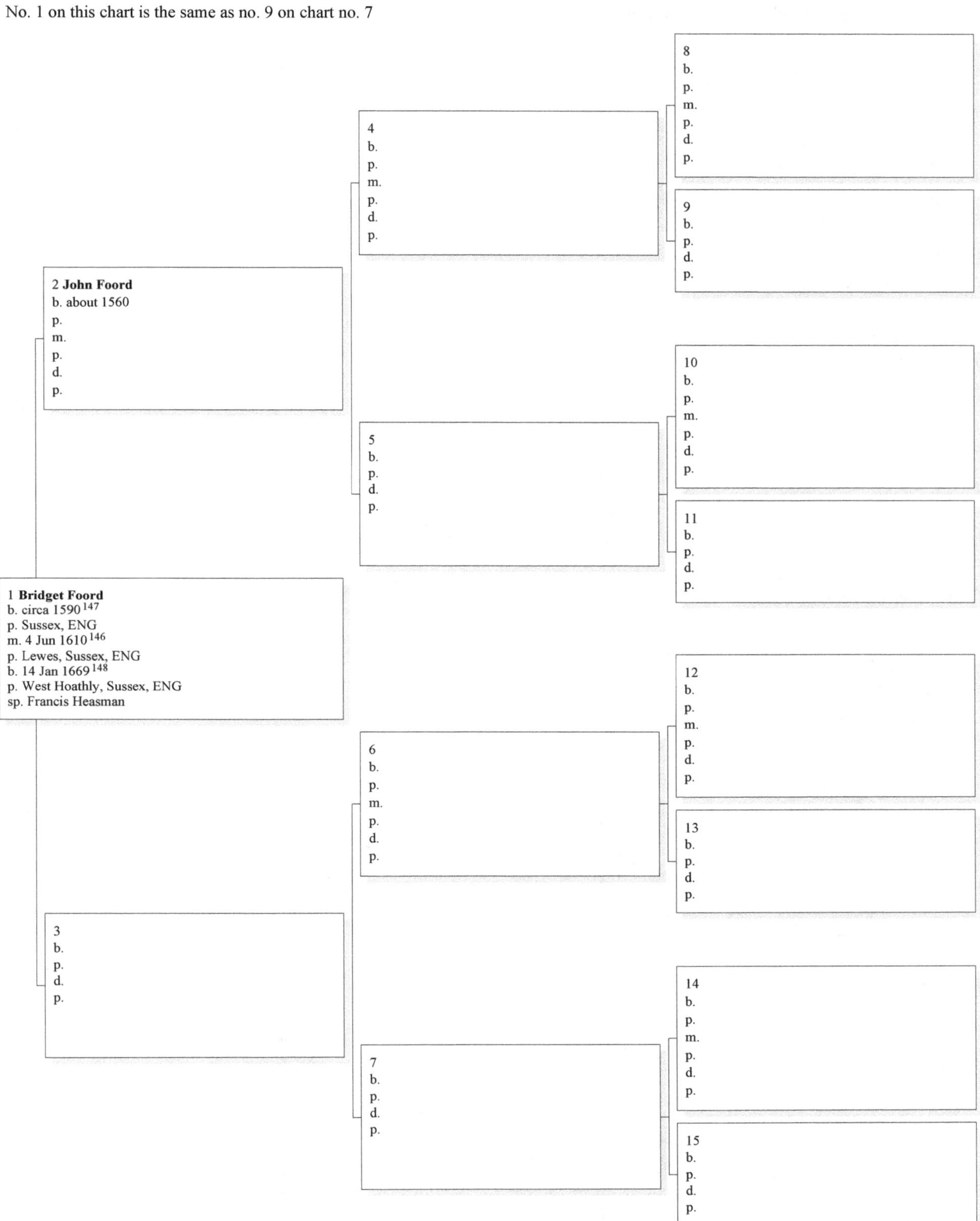

Ancestor Chart for Frederick Keith Heasman

No. 1 on this chart is the same as no. 9 on chart no. 7

Ancestor Chart for Frederick Keith Heasman

No. 1 on this chart is the same as no. 13 on chart no. 10

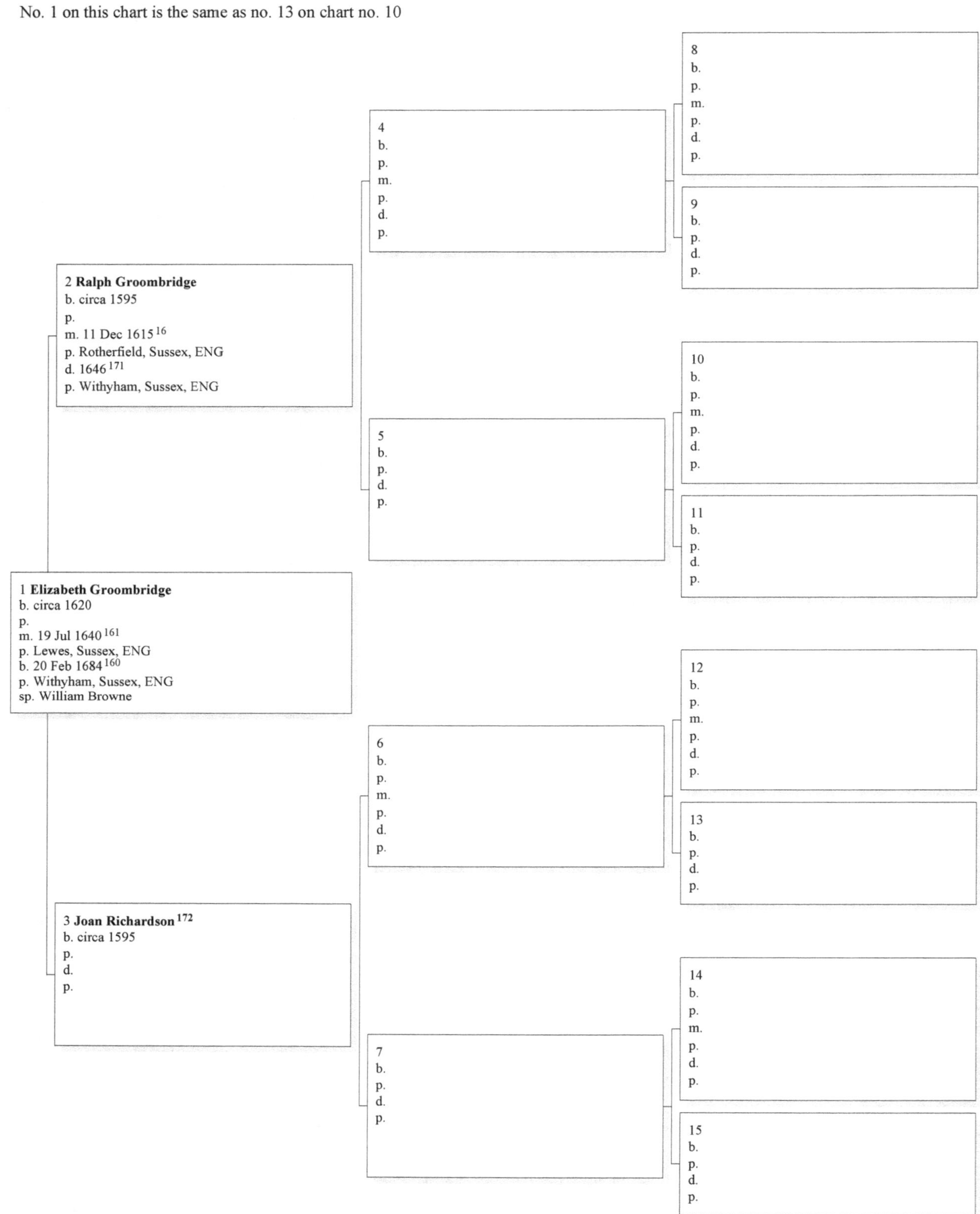

Ancestor Chart for Frederick Keith Heasman

No. 1 on this chart is the same as no. 8 on chart no. 14

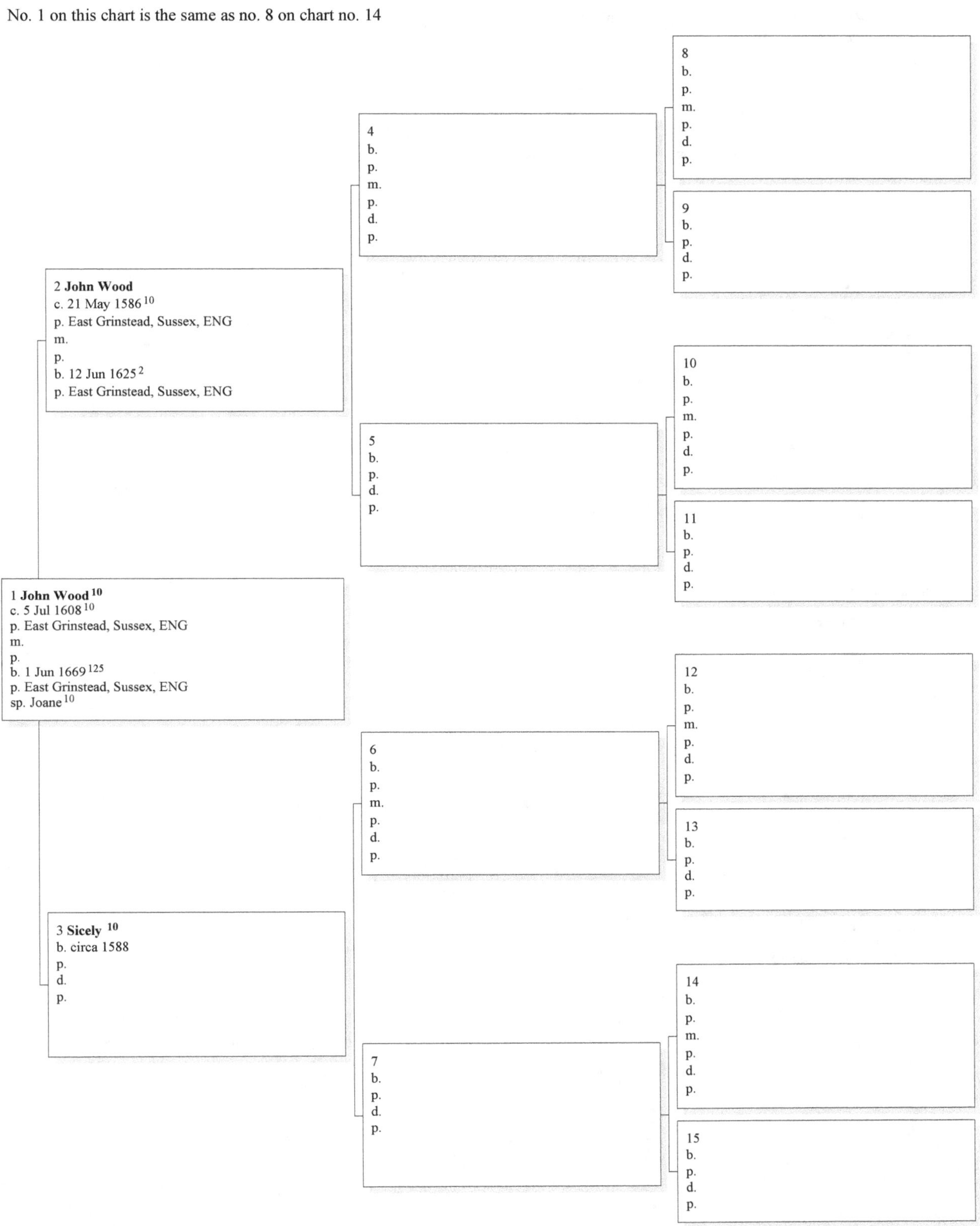

Ancestor Chart for Frederick Keith Heasman

No. 1 on this chart is the same as no. 10 on chart no. 14

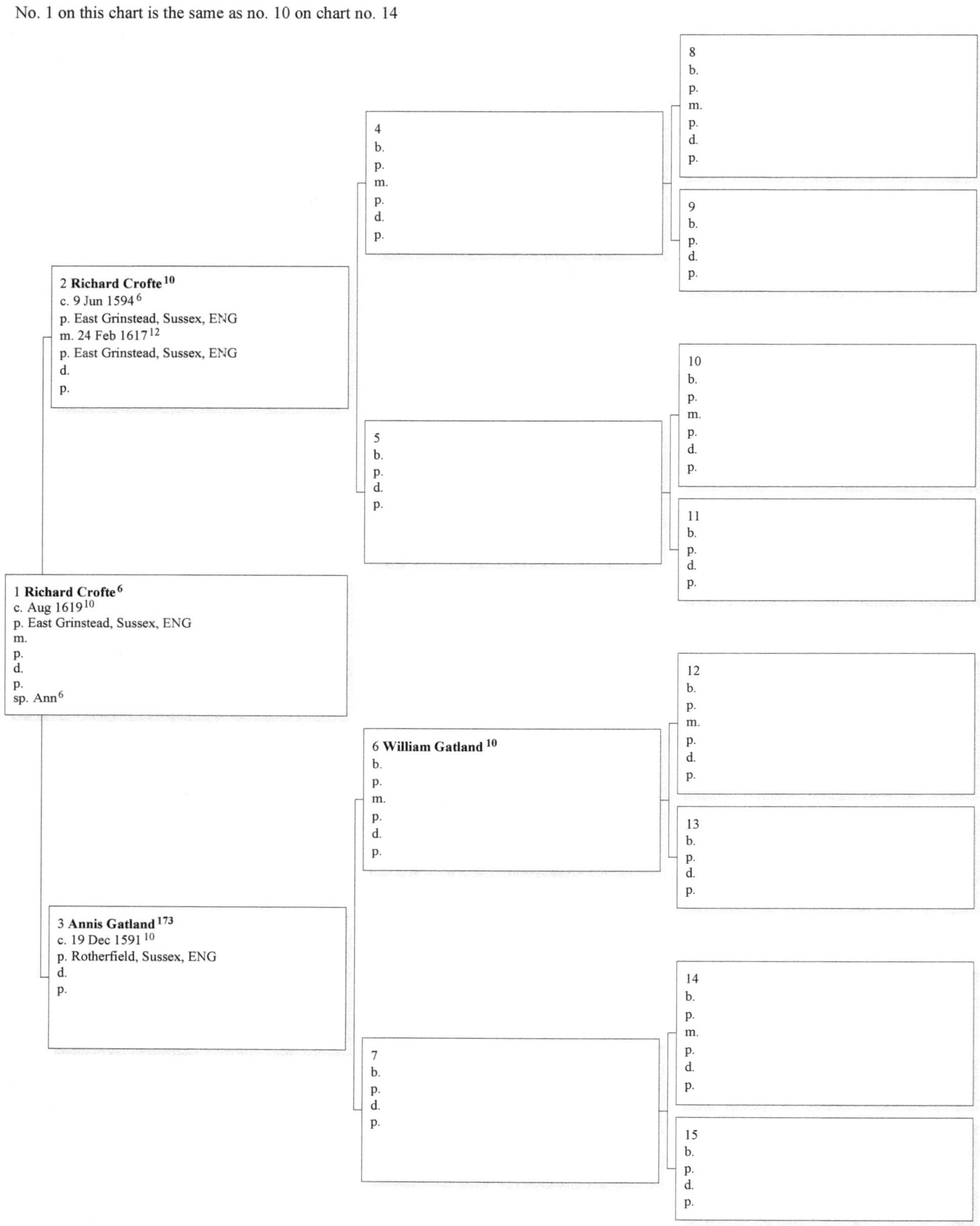

Ancestor Report for Frederick Keith Heasman

First Generation

Keith Heasman

1. Frederick Keith Heasman, son of **Frederick Huston "F. H." Heasman**[46] and **Elinor "Nellie" Kerr,** was born on 27 Sep 1898 in West Springfield, Erie, Pennsylvania,[116] died on 27 Feb 1960 in Conneaut, Ashtabula, Ohio[117] at age 61, and was buried in Glenwood Cemetery, Conneaut, Ashtabula, Ohio. Another name for Frederick was Wimp.

General Notes: Both of Fred and Marion Heasman's sons worked in Heasman's Grocery Store, which was originally located on State Street, and later on Main & Mill St., in Conneaut. According to Laura Jane Heasman's published account: "Two sons were born who carried on the business having learned the business from youth. Frederick Keith learned to be manager of the grocery department and Darrell Esmond learned to run the meat department and was a first class meat cutter and manager of the meat department." According to his daughter Patricia Heasman, Keith Heasman continued to work at Heasman's Grocery until he died in 1960. He passed away at home on his lunch break.[174]

Noted events in his life were:
- Resided: 1900, Conneaut, Ashtabula, Ohio.[53]

- Resided: 1910, Conneaut, Ashtabula, Ohio.[49]

- Occupation: a grocer at Heasman's Grocery Store, 1918, Conneaut, Ashtabula, Ohio.[116]

- Military: WW I draft registration, Sep 1918, Ashtabula, Ohio.[116]

- Article: from the Conneaut News-Herald, 1919, Conneaut, Ashtabula, Ohio.[175]

- Occupation: manager of the Quality Cash Store at 278 Main Street, 1919, Conneaut, Ashtabula, Ohio.[175]

- Resided: 1920, Conneaut, Ashtabula, Ohio.[58]

- Resided: 216 Mill on Heasman's Block 378-386 Main, 1930, Conneaut, Ashtabula, Ohio.[176]

- Resided: 216 Mill, 1940, Conneaut, Ashtabula, Ohio.[60]

- Article: Notice of Keith Heasman's death, 1960, Conneaut, Ashtabula, Ohio.[177]

Frederick married **Marion Katherine Rodgers,** daughter of **Clarence Frederick "C. F." Rodgers D. D. S.**[178] and **Katherine Margaret "Kit" Nellis,** on 22 Jul 1919 in Conneaut, Ashtabula, Ohio.[118]

Marion K. Rodgers

Noted events in her life were:
- Resided: 1900, Conneaut, Ashtabula, Ohio.[53]

- Education: trained as a milliner, before 1918, Buffalo, Erie, New York.[179]

- Resided: 1920, Conneaut, Ashtabula, Ohio.[58]

- Resided: 1930, Conneaut, Ashtabula, Ohio.[107]

- Occupation: co-owner of Heasman's grocery store, about 1960.[179]

- Obituary: The Star Beacon, 1992, Ashtabula, Ashtabula, Ohio.[180]

Ancestor Report for Frederick Keith Heasman

Ancestor Report for Frederick Keith Heasman

Second Generation (Parents)

2. Frederick Huston "F. H." Heasman,[46] son of **Thomas Heasman** and **Emily "Emma" Stubbs,** was born on 29 Oct 1869 in New Alresford, Hampshire, England,[47] died on 6 May 1952 in Conneaut, Ashtabula, Ohio[46] at age 82, and was buried in Glenwood Cemetery, Conneaut, Ashtabula, Ohio.

F.H. Heasman

> General Notes: F.H. Heasman was born in England, immigrated with his family to Canada at the age of four, and immigrated to America at the age of twenty-five. He raised his family in Conneaut, Ohio, where he became a noted merchant and entrepreneur best known for his property called the Heasman Block and for Heasman's Grocery. He married twice: first to Nellie Kerr with whom he had his children Keith and Darrell, and second to Gertrude Zundel. [48]

Noted events in his life were:
- Immigration: 1873, Canada.[49]

- Occupation: woolen weaver, 1891, Cobourg, Northumberland, Ontario, Canada. [27]

- Occupation: railroad worker, barge worker, tugboat worker, before 1894, Canada. [50]

- Immigration: 1894, Pennsylvania.[51]

- Resided: 1894, Harris, Ontario, Canada. [52]

- Occupation: merchant, 1900, Conneaut, Ashtabula, Ohio. [53]

- Resided: at 420 Buffalo Street, 1908, Conneaut, Ashtabula, Ohio. [54]

- Occupation: store owner, 1910, Conneaut, Ashtabula, Ohio. [55]

- Resided: at 378 1/2 Main Street, 1912, Conneaut, Ashtabula, Ohio. [54]

- Occupation: owner, Heasman Grocery, 382-394 Main St., 1916, Conneaut, Ashtabula, Ohio.[56]

- Resided: Heasman Block (former Baldwin Block), 1916, Conneaut, Ashtabula, Ohio. [56]

- Article: marriage notice in Conneaut News-Herald, 16 Sep 1919, Conneaut, Ashtabula, Ohio.[57]

- Occupation: grocery store owner, 1920, Conneaut, Ashtabula, Ohio. [58]

- Bio: From History of Ashtabula County, 1924.[42]

- Occupation: manager of general store, The Heasman Co., 380-386 Main (Heasmans Block), 1930, Conneaut, Ashtabula, Ohio.[59]

- Resided: 378 Main, 1940, Conneaut, Ashtabula, Ohio. [60]

- Bio: Ashtabula County History, Then and Now, 1985.[61]

- Bio: Patricia Heasman oral history, 2002.[48]

Frederick married **Elinor "Nellie" Kerr** on 7 Aug 1894 in Corry, Erie, Pennsylvania.[52]

> Marriage Notes: She and her sister Jennie were married one day apart in Corry, Erie, Pennsylvania.

Children from this marriage were:

    1   i.   **Frederick Keith Heasman**

ii. **Darrell Esmond "Red" Heasman** was born on 12 Feb 1901 in Conneaut, Ashtabula, Ohio[181] and died in 1954 in Conneaut, Ashtabula, Ohio[182] at age 53.

Frederick next married **Gertrude Zundel,** daughter of **Robert H. Zundel**[53] and **Emma V. Tucker,**[65] on 13 Sep 1919 in Conneaut, Ashtabula, Ohio.[64]

Gertrude Zundel

Noted events in her life were:
- Occupation: bookkeeper Heasman's Grocery.[68]

- Resided: 1900, Jamestown, Mercer, Pennsylvania.[53]

- Occupation: bookkeeper in department store, 1910, Conneaut, Ashtabula, Ohio.[49]

- Obituary: from Conneaut News-Herald, 14 Jun 1972, Conneaut, Ashtabula, Ohio.[69]

3. Elinor "Nellie" Kerr, daughter of **Andrew Kerr** and **Jane Allingham,** was born on 19 Mar 1870 in Baltimore, Hamilton, Northumberland, Ontario, Canada,[62] died on 30 May 1918 in Conneaut, Ashtabula, Ohio[63] at age 48, and was buried on 2 Jun 1918 in Glenwood Cemetery, Conneaut, Ashtabula, Ohio.[46]

Nellie Kerr

General Notes: Nellie Kerr's parents and eldest sister were born in Ireland and Nellie was born in Canada. She moved with two sisters, Jennie and Lottie, from their farm in Hamilton Township, Ontario, to nearby Cobourg where she worked as a dressmaker. Nellie married F.H. Heasman in Erie County, Pennsylvania and settled in Conneaut, Ohio. They had two children.

Noted events in her life were:
- Resided: 1881, Hamilton Township, Northumberland, Ontario, Canada.[26]

- Religion: Methodist, 1891.[27]

- Resided: lodger, 1891, Cobourg, Northumberland, Ontario, Canada.[27]

- Resided: 1894, Erie, Erie, Pennsylvania.[52]

- Resided: 1900, Conneaut, Ashtabula, Ohio.[53]

- Resided: at 452 State St., 1910, Conneaut, Ashtabula, Ohio.[55]

Elinor married **Frederick Huston "F. H." Heasman**[46] on 7 Aug 1894 in Corry, Erie, Pennsylvania.[52]

Ancestor Report for Frederick Keith Heasman

Third Generation (Grandparents)

4. Thomas Heasman, son of **Samuel Heasman** and **Sarah Shoebridge,** was born on 20 Feb 1839 in Hartfield, Sussex, England,[14] was baptized on 24 Mar 1839 in Saint Mary the Virgin Church, Hartfield, Sussex, England,[1] and died on 17 Apr 1916 in Cobourg, Northumberland, Ontario, Canada[14] at age 77.

General Notes:

Thomas Heasman left his home in Hartfield, England where he was a farm laborer and moved fifty miles west to Ropley village near the town of Alresford (pronounced "Alsford"), Hampshire County (abbreviated "Hants"). He worked for Mid-Hants Railway Company, which in 1861 had started work on a railway through Ropley connecting to London. The new railway, which was completed in 1865, allowed watercress farmers in the area to ship fresh watercress to London. A portion of the railway is still open and operates as the "Watercress Line."

In the early 1870s, the government of Ontario, Canada distributed flyers to workers in England encouraging immigration. Thomas Heasman and his family boarded a sailing vessel bound for Quebec in 1873. The trip took six weeks, and upon arrival they moved to Cobourg, Ontario, a small town southwest of Kingston on the north shore of Lake Ontario.

Thomas Heasman found employment as a railroad worker with the Grand Trunk Railway. The original Grand Trunk line was completed in 1856 and connected Montreal to Toronto. In 1873 the Grand Trunk Railway Company continued to extend the line and began converting existing track to the "Standard" gauge. Thomas Heasman worked for the railroad for a time, then took up farming and later became a milk dealer in Cobourg, Canada.

Noted events in his life were:

- Resided: 1841, Graddock's Pit, Hartfield, Sussex, England.[3]

- Occupation: farm laborer, 1851, Graddock's Pit, Hartfield, Sussex, England.[4]

- Occupation: railway platelayer (track maintenance), 1871, New Alresford, Hampshire, England.[18]

- Immigration: 1873, Canada.

- Occupation: laborer, 1881, Cobourg, Northumberland, Ontario, Canada.[26]

- Religion: Bible Christian (Wesleyan Methodist), 1881.[26]

- Occupation: farmer, 1891, Cobourg, Northumberland, Ontario, Canada.[27]

- Religion: 1891, Methodist.[27]

- Occupation: milk dealer, 1901, Cobourg, Northumberland, Ontario, Canada.[28]

- Resided: 1911, Cobourg, Northumberland, Ontario, Canada.[29]

- Cause of death: suddenly from heart disease.

Thomas married **Emily "Emma" Stubbs** on 16 Dec 1865 in Ropley, Hampshire, England.[15]

Children from this marriage were:

	i.	**Frank Heasman** was born on 23 Oct 1867 in New Alresford, Hampshire, England.[35]
2	ii.	**Frederick Huston "F. H." Heasman**[46]
	iii.	**Fannie Heasman** was born on 30 Jan 1872 in New Alresford, Hampshire, England,[27] died on 1 Feb 1942[70] at age 70, and was buried in Mount Pleasant Cemetery, Toronto, Ontario, Canada.[70]
	iv.	**William Heasman** was born on 16 May 1874 in Cobourg, Northumberland,

Ontario, Canada,[71] died on 12 Feb 1969 in Victoria, British Columbia, Canada[72] at age 94, and was buried in Saanich, British Columbia, Canada.[72]

    v.   **Alberta Heasman** was born on 23 Jul 1878 in Cobourg, Northumberland, Ontario, Canada[27] and died in 1929 in California[77] at age 51.

    vi.   **Sgt. Ernest Almer "E.A." Heasman** was born on 13 Jun 1887 in Cobourg, Northumberland, Ontario, Canada.[80]

Emma Stubbs

5. Emily "Emma" Stubbs, daughter of **Henry Stubbs** and **Sarah Paice,** was born on 30 Nov 1842 in Ropley, Hampshire, England,[30] was baptized on 11 Dec 1842 in Ropley, Hampshire, England,[7] died on 19 Mar 1928 in York, Ontario, Canada[31] at age 85, and was buried on 21 Mar 1928 in Cobourg, Northumberland, Ontario, Canada.[32]

General Notes: As a teenager Emma Stubbs worked as a servant at the home of retired navy commander Lt. Charles Batten in the East End Villa of West Meon, Hampshire, England. The Battans had two servants: Emma. the cook, and Ann Upsdale, the house maid. Emma married Thomas Heasman in 1865 and immigrated to Canada with her husband and three children in 1873. They settled in Cobourg where they had three more children. After Thomas died in 1916 she moved in with her son Frank in New Liskeard, Ontario.

Noted events in her life were:
- Occupation: cook in the Charles Batten home, 1861, West Meon, Hampshire, England.[9]

- Resided: 1871, New Alresford, Hampshire, England.[18]

- Resided: 1891, Cobourg, Northumberland, Ontario, Canada.[27]

- Resided: 1911, Cobourg, Northumberland, Ontario, Canada.[29]

- Boarder Crossing: 15 Jun 1918, Buffalo, Erie, New York.[33]

- Resided: 1921, New Liskeard, Temiskaming, Ontario, Canada.[34]

Emily married **Thomas Heasman** on 16 Dec 1865 in Ropley, Hampshire, England.[15]

6. Andrew Kerr, son of **George Kerr**[14] and **Jane,** was born about 8 May 1838 in Fermanagh, Ireland[95] and died on 8 Jun 1910 in Cobourg, Northumberland, Ontario, Canada[14] about age 72.

Noted events in his life were:
- Religion: Church Of Ireland (Methodist).

- Famine: 1845-1851, Fermanagh, Ireland.

- Occupation: laborer, 1859, Derrygonnelly, Fermanagh, Ireland.

- Immigration: on the steamship Jura, 1 Apr 1862, Portland and Falmouth, Maine.[28]

- Occupation: farmer, 1881, Hamilton Township, Northumberland, Ontario, Canada.[26]

- Occupation: farmer, 1891, Hamilton Township, Northumberland, Ontario, Canada.[27]

- Resided: 1901, Port Hope, Durham, Ontario, Canada.[101]

Andrew married **Jane Allingham** on 23 Jun 1859 in Saint Ninnidhs Church, Binmore Glebe, Fermanagh, Ireland.[96]

Marriage Notes:
"Andrew Kerr of full age, bachelor and labourer of Derrygonnelly, son of George Kerr, labourer, married Jane Allingham of full age, spinster of Drumdoonian, daughter of John Allingham, labourer, on 23 June

Ancestor Report for Frederick Keith Heasman

1859." The bride and groom signed the certificate with Xs.

Children from this marriage were:

      i.   **Margaret Jane "Jennie" Kerr** was born on 13 Feb 1861 in Derrygonnelly, Fermanagh, Ireland[105] and died on 20 Aug 1937 in Millcreek, Erie, Pennsylvania[106] at age 76.

      ii.   **Mary Ann Kerr** was born circa 1863 in Ontario, Canada.[110]

      iii.   **William George Kerr** was born on 22 Aug 1868 in Clarke, Ontario, Canada[112] and died on 5 Nov 1926 in Cobourg, Northumberland, Ontario, Canada[14] at age 58.

3   iv.   **Elinor "Nellie" Kerr**

      v.   **Charlotte Elizabeth "Lottie" Kerr** was born circa 1880 in Ontario, Canada.[26]

Andrew next married **Ann Jane Coomb,** daughter of **Thomas Coomb**[111] and **Jane,**[111] on 13 Nov 1884 in Port Hope, Durham, Ontario, Canada.[97]

7. Jane Allingham, daughter of **John Allingham,** was born circa 1839 in Ireland[102] and died on 10 Feb 1884 in Hamilton Township, Northumberland, Ontario, Canada[14] about age 45. The cause of her death was tumor in stomach.

Birth Notes: Jane's recorded birth year ranges from 1838 to 1841.

Noted events in her life were:
• Resided: 1859, Fermanagh, Ireland.[103]

• Immigration: on the steamship Jura, 1 Apr 1862, Portland and Falmouth, Maine.[28]

• Resided: 1871, Hamilton Township, Northumberland, Ontario, Canada.[104]

• Resided: 1881, Hamilton Township, Northumberland, Ontario, Canada.[26]

Jane married **Andrew Kerr** on 23 Jun 1859 in Saint Ninnidhs Church, Binmore Glebe, Fermanagh, Ireland.[96]

Ancestor Report for Frederick Keith Heasman

Fourth Generation (Great-Grandparents)

8. Samuel Heasman, son of **James Heasman** and **Elizabeth Turk,** was baptized on 9 Jun 1799 in Saint Mary the Virgin Church, Hartfield, Sussex, England[1] and was buried on 28 Feb 1855 in East Grinstead, Sussex, England.[2]

> General Notes: Samuel Heasman was an agricultural laborer. He lived with his wife and children in a cottage at Graddock's Pit Farm at Graddock's Pit Wood. Graddock's Pit, also called Cabbagestalk, lies between Ten Acre Wood and Paternoster Wood in West Hartfield. His brothers Thomas and Henry lived next door with his in-laws in the 1830s and 1840s.

Noted events in his life were:
- Occupation: agricultural laborer, 1841, Graddock's Pit, Hartfield, Sussex, England.[3]

- Occupation: agricultural laborer, 1851, Graddock's Pit, Hartfield, Sussex, England.[4]

Samuel married **Sarah Shoebridge** on 2 Oct 1824 in Saint Swithuns, East Grinstead, Sussex, England.[5]

Children from this marriage were:

    i.   **Harriett Heasman** was baptized on 2 Oct 1825 in Hartfield, Sussex, England,[10] died on 4 Feb 1866 at age 40, and was buried on 4 Feb 1866 in Withyham, Sussex, England.[5]

    ii.   **Philadelphia Heasman** was baptized on 29 Mar 1829 in Hartfield, Sussex, England[11] and died circa Feb 1903 in East Grinstead, Sussex, England[11] about age 73.

    iii.   **Jane Heasman** was baptized on 30 Oct 1831 in Hartfield, Sussex, England[10] and died circa Feb 1909 in Sevenoaks, Kent, England[11] about age 77.

    iv.   **Jesse Heasman** was baptized on 22 Jun 1834 in Hartfield, Sussex, England.[13]

    v.   **Mary Ann Heasman** was baptized on 25 Sep 1836 in Saint Mary the Virgin Church, Hartfield, Sussex, England.[10]

4   vi.   **Thomas Heasman**

    vii.   **Ann Heasman** was baptized on 9 Jan 1842 in Saint Mary the Virgin Church, Hartfield, Sussex, England[10] and died circa Aug 1920 in East Grinstead, Sussex, England[11] about age 78.

    viii.   **Hannah Heasman** was born circa Feb 1845 in Hartfield, Sussex, England,[17] was baptized on 16 Jan 1848 in Saint Mary the Virgin Church, Hartfield, Sussex, England,[10] and died in 1891 in Kensington, London, England[11] about age 46.

    ix.   **Emily Heasman** was born in 1848 in Hartfield, Sussex, England[9] and was baptized on 16 Jan 1848 in Saint Mary the Virgin Church, Hartfield, Sussex, England.[1]

9. Sarah Shoebridge, daughter of **Jesse Shoebridge**[6] and **Karen "Carey" Weller,** was baptized on 20 Apr 1806 in Hartfield, Sussex, England[7] and died circa Feb 1872 in Sussex, England[8] about age 65.

Noted events in her life were:
- Resided: at Graddock's Pit farm, 1841, Hartfield, Sussex, England.[3]

- Resided: at Graddock's Pit farm, 1851, Hartfield, Sussex, England.[4]

- Resided: at Marsh Green, 1861, Hartfield, Sussex, England.[9]

Sarah married **Samuel Heasman** on 2 Oct 1824 in Saint Swithuns, East Grinstead, Sussex, England.[5]

10. Henry Stubbs, son of **James Stubbs**[12] and **Mary Wateridge,** was baptized on 11 Aug 1816 in Ropley, Hampshire, England[83] and died in Apr 1891 in West Battersea, London, England[84] at age 74.

> General Notes: Henry Stubbs was a carter (delivered goods on an ox- or horse-drawn wagon) and agricultural laborer. The main agricultural crop in the area was watercress. He moved several times among neighboring villages. In his retirement he moved to London to live with his daughter, Frances.

Noted events in his life were:
- Occupation: agricultural laborer residing on North Street, 1841, Ropley, Hampshire, England.[3]

- Occupation: agricultural laborer residing at Ropley Soke, 1851, Ropley, Hampshire, England.[4]

- Occupation: carter, 1861, Ropley, Hampshire, England.[9]

- Occupation: agricultural laborer, 1871, Bishops Sutton, Alresford, Hampshire, England.[18]

- Occupation: agricultural laborer residing at Sutton Wood Cottages, 1881, Bishops Sutton, Alresford, Hampshire, England.[19]

- Resided: widowed and living with his daughter Frances, 5 Apr 1891, West Battersea, London, England.[25]

Henry married **Sarah Paice** on 29 Feb 1840 in West Tisted, Hampshire, England.[15]

Children from this marriage were:

	i.	**Mary Ann Stubbs** was born circa 1840 in Ropley, Hampshire, England[86] and died circa Nov 1870 in Alton, Hampshire, England[87] about age 30.
	ii.	**Stubbs** was born about 1841.[3]
	iii.	**Frances "Fanny" Stubbs** was baptized on 14 May 1841 in Ropley, Hampshire, England[21] and died in Mar 1924 in London, England[32] at age 82.
5	iv.	**Emily "Emma" Stubbs**
	v.	**Elizabeth Stubbs** was baptized on 11 Aug 1844 in Ropley, Hampshire, England.[7]

11. Sarah Paice, daughter of **William Paice**[15] and **Hannah Aldred,** was baptized on 17 Jan 1819 in West Tisted, Hampshire, England[10] and died circa May 1889 in Alresford, Hampshire, England[11] about age 70.

Noted events in her life were:
- Resided: on North Street, 1841, Ropley, Hampshire, England.[3]

- Resided: 1851, Bishops Waltham, Hampshire, England.[4]

- Resided: on Lymington Bottom, 1861, Ropley, Hampshire, England.[9]

- Resided: on Ranscombe Farm, 1871, Bishops Sutton, Alresford, Hampshire, England.[18]

- Resided: at Sutton Wood Cottages, 1881, Bishops Sutton, Alresford, Hampshire, England.[19]

Sarah married **Henry Stubbs** on 29 Feb 1840 in West Tisted, Hampshire, England.[15]

12. George Kerr,[14] son of **George Kerr** and **Margaret Eaton,** was born in Carrick, Fermanagh, Ireland[91] and was baptized on 13 Jan 1814 in Upper Inishmacsaint, Fermanagh, Ireland. [91]

> Christening Notes: Their church was in the village of Drumenagh, also called Church Hill. The church was built in 1688.

> General Notes: He is listed as landowner in Griffith Valuations, along with Robert, Thomas, and John of Carrick, who may have been his brothers or sons. He rented from Mervyn Edward Archdale, MP a house with yard and garden on Main street in Derrygonnelly, as well as a small parcel of land near John Allingham in Sandhill.

> Noted events in his life were:
> • Resided: at 44 Main St., 1862, Derrygonnelly, Fermanagh, Ireland. [92]

George married **Jane** about 1835 in Ireland.[93]

Children from this marriage were:

	i.	**Thomas Kerr**[28] was born on 14 Aug 1837 in Fermanagh, Ireland,[94] died on 13 Nov 1904[70] at age 67, and was buried in Saint John's Anglican Church Cemetery, Port Hope, Northumberland, Ontario, Canada.
6	ii.	**Andrew Kerr**

13. Jane.

Jane married **George Kerr**[14] about 1835 in Ireland.[93]

14. John Allingham was born about 1810.

> Research Notes: John Allingham is listed as a landholder in Sandhill near Derrygonnelly in Griffith Valuations. He sublet his home from Alexander Acheson and leased 65 acres from Mervyn Edward Archdale, MP.

> Noted events in his life were:
> • Land: 1862, Sandhill, Fermanagh, Ireland.[115]

John married someone.

His child was:

7	i.	**Jane Allingham**

Ancestor Report for Frederick Keith Heasman

Ancestor Report for Frederick Keith Heasman

Fifth Generation (Great Great-Grandparents)

16. James Heasman, son of **Samuel Heasman** and **Sarah Wheatley,** was baptized on 30 Jul 1775 in Saint Swithuns, East Grinstead, Sussex, England[10] and died circa Feb 1859 in Sussex, England[8] about age 83.

> Research Notes: His children were not baptized in the Church of England; those born after 1801 were registered on the Nonconformist Register on 1st Sep 1814. They may have been Wesleyan Methodists.

Noted events in his life were:
- Occupation: agricultural laborer, 1841, Ashdown Forest, East Grinstead, Sussex, England. [3]

- Resided: at Quabrook at Parrock Lane just north of Coleman's Hatch, 1851, East Grinstead, Sussex, England.[4]

James married **Elizabeth Turk** on 2 Nov 1797 in Saint Swithuns, East Grinstead, Sussex, England.[12]

Children from this marriage were:

8	i.	**Samuel Heasman**
	ii.	**Thomas Heasman** was baptized on 1 Mar 1801 in Saint Mary the Virgin Church, Hartfield, Sussex, England[10] and was buried on 23 Mar 1871 in Saint Mary the Virgin Church, Hartfield, Sussex, England.[8]
	iii.	**Sarah Heasman** was born on 20 Mar 1802 in Hartfield, Sussex, England. [183]
	iv.	**Susanna Heasman** was born on 10 Dec 1804 in Hartfield, Sussex, England[184] and was buried in Jul 1844 in Cuckfield, Sussex, England.[8]
	v.	**Henry Heasman** was born on 12 Jul 1806 in Little Parrock Farm, Hartfield, Sussex, England[185] and died in Nov 1893 in East Grinstead, Sussex, England[11] at age 87.
	vi.	**Solomon Heasman** was born on 11 Mar 1808 in East Grinstead, Sussex, England[185] and died on 25 May 1831 in East Grinstead, Sussex, England[2] at age 23.
	vii.	**Mary Ann Heasman** was born on 5 Apr 1810 in East Grinstead, Sussex, England[186] and was baptized on 5 Aug 1827 in Saint Mary the Virgin Church, Hartfield, Sussex, England.[187]
	viii.	**Lucy Heasman** was born on 15 Nov 1811 in East Grinstead, Sussex, England,[185] was baptized on 1 Jun 1828 in Saint Mary the Virgin Church, Hartfield, Sussex, England,[10] and died circa Feb 1883 in Islington, Middlesex, England[8] about age 71.

17. Elizabeth Turk, daughter of **Thomas Turk** and **Mary,** was baptized on 11 Apr 1779 in Saint Peters Church, Pembury, Kent, England[10] and was buried on 6 Jul 1845 in Hartfield, Sussex, England.[2]

Noted events in her life were:
- Resided: 1841, Ashdown Forest, East Grinstead, Sussex, England. [3]

Elizabeth married **James Heasman** on 2 Nov 1797 in Saint Swithuns, East Grinstead, Sussex, England.[12]

18. Jesse Shoebridge,[6] son of **John Shoebridge**[7] and **Elizabeth Wood,**[131] was baptized on 21 Jul 1776 in Hartfield, Sussex, England[127] and was buried on 1 Feb 1848 in Hartfield, Sussex, England.[2]

Ancestor Report for Frederick Keith Heasman

Research Notes: In the draft list he is "labourer and willing to serve." (In 1803 Napoleon threatened invasion of England led to an Act of Parliament to identify those men who could be co-opted into a defense force. Lists were drawn up of all men between the ages of 17 and 55.)

Noted events in his life were:
- Occupation: agricultural laborer, 1841, Lower Pest House, No 2, Hartfield, , Sussex, England.[3]

Jesse married **Karen "Carey" Weller** on 19 Mar 1803 in Hartfield, Sussex, England.[129]

Children from this marriage were:

    i.   **John Shoebridge** was born in 1803 in Hartfield, Sussex, England,[128] was baptized on 29 May 1803 in Saint Mary the Virgin Church, Hartfield, Sussex, England,[1] and was buried on 30 Aug 1881 in Saint Mary the Virgin Church, Hartfield, Sussex, England.[187]

    ii.   **Mary Shoebridge** was born in 1805 in Hartfield, Sussex, England[128] and was baptized on 5 Mar 1805 in Hartfield, Sussex, England.[1]

9   iii.   **Sarah Shoebridge**

    iv.   **Philadelphia Shoebridge** was born in 1808 in Hartfield, Sussex, England,[128] was baptized on 11 Sep 1808 in Hartfield, Sussex, England,[1] and died circa Jul 1884 in East Grinstead, Sussex, England[8] about age 76.

    v.   **Jane Shoebridge** was baptized on 16 Feb 1812 in Hartfield, Sussex, England[10] and died circa Aug 1846 in East Grinstead, Sussex, England[8] about age 34.

    vi.   **Harriet Shoebridge** was born in 1816 in Hartfield, Sussex, England,[128] was baptized on 21 Jan 1816 in Hartfield, Sussex, England,[1] and died in Missouri.[70]

    vii.   **Mary Ann Shoebridge** was born in 1819 in Hartfield, Sussex, England,[128] was baptized on 4 Apr 1819 in Hartfield, Sussex, England,[10] and died in 1892 in Cooper, Missouri[70] at age 73.

19. Karen "Carey" Weller, daughter of **William Weller**[1] and **Sarah Andrews,** was baptized on 19 Jun 1774 in Saint Martin of Tours Church, Ashurst, Kent, England[1] and was buried on 5 May 1860 in Hartfield, Sussex, England.[130]

Noted events in her life were:
- Resided: Lower Pest House, No 2, 1841, Hartfield, Sussex, England.[3]

- Resided: Mill Bank, as a widow with her daughter Harriet, 1851, Hartfield, Sussex, England.[4]

Karen married **Jesse Shoebridge**[6] on 19 Mar 1803 in Hartfield, Sussex, England.[129]

20. James Stubbs,[12] son of **John Stubbs** and **Elizabeth Budd,** was born in 1782 in Ropley, Hampshire, England and was buried on 10 Feb 1860 in Ropley, Hampshire, England.[125]

Noted events in his life were:
- Occupation: agricultural laborer living at North Street, 1841, Ropley, Hampshire, England.[3]

- Resided: agricultural laborer living on Gilbert Street, 1851, Ropley, Hampshire, England.[4]

James married **Mary Wateridge** on 6 Jun 1808 in Ropley, Hampshire, England.[15]

Children from this marriage were:

    i.   **John Stubbs** was born on 9 Feb 1810,[10] was baptized on 8 Apr 1810 in Ropley,

Hampshire, England,[10] and died circa Aug 1880 in Alresford, Hampshire, England[8] about age 70.

    ii.   **James Stubbs** was born on 10 Mar 1812 in Ropley, Hampshire, England,[10] was baptized on 12 Apr 1812 in Ropley, Hampshire, England,[10] and died circa May 1890 in Alresford, Hampshire, England[8] about age 78.

10   iii.   **Henry Stubbs**

21. Mary Wateridge, daughter of **Richard Wateridge** and **Elizabeth Pink,** was baptized on 26 May 1784 in Medstead, Hampshire, England,[10] died circa Jul 1865 in Alresford, Hampshire, England[132] about age 81, and was buried on 6 Aug 1865 in Ropley, Hampshire, England. [125]

Noted events in her life were:
- Resided: at North Street, 1841, Ropley, Hampshire, England.[3]

- Resided: on Gilbert Street, 1851, Ropley, Hampshire, England.[4]

Mary married **James Stubbs**[12] on 6 Jun 1808 in Ropley, Hampshire, England.[15]

22. William Paice[15] was born circa 1783 in West Tisted, Hampshire, England[4] and was buried on 4 Dec 1853 in West Tisted, Hampshire, England. [125]

Research Notes: His parents were probably Henry and Mary Paice, based on the other children born around the same time in West Tisted.

Noted events in his life were:
- Resided: on a stock farm, 1841, West Tisted, Hampshire, England.[3]

- Occupation: agricultural laborer on common farm, 1851, West Tisted, Hampshire, England.[4]

William married **Hannah Aldred** on 22 Oct 1804 in Froxfield, Hampshire, England.[16]

Children from this marriage were:

    i.   **Frances Paice** was born on 14 Apr 1805 in Froxfield, Hampshire, England[6] and was baptized on 28 Apr 1805 in Froxfield, Hampshire, England.[6]

    ii.   **William Paice** was baptized on 25 Feb 1810 in West Tisted, Hampshire, England.[10]

   iii.   **Lydia Paice** was baptized on 22 Mar 1812 in West Tisted, Hampshire, England. [10]

   iv.   **Peter Paice** was baptized on 10 Apr 1814 in West Tisted, Hampshire, England[10] and was buried on 12 Mar 1852 in West Tisted, Hampshire, England. [125]

    v.   **Mary Paice** was baptized on 25 Dec 1816 in West Tisted, Hampshire, England. [10]

11   vi.   **Sarah Paice**

   vii.   **Elizabeth Paice** was baptized on 16 Sep 1821 in West Tisted, Hampshire, England[10] and died in Oct 1890 in Hampshire, England[8] at age 69.

  viii.   **Dinah Paice** was baptized on 28 Dec 1823 in West Tisted, Hampshire, England. [10]

   ix.   **Stephen Paice** was baptized on 4 Feb 1827 in West Tisted, Hampshire, England[10] and died in 1896 in Hampshire, England[8] at age 69.

    x.   **James Paice** was baptized on 13 Jun 1830 in West Tisted, Hampshire, England. [10]

23. Hannah Aldred, daughter of **Mary Aldred,** was born on 19 May 1786,[137] was baptized on 27 May 1786 in All Saints Church, Steep, Hampshire, England,[140] and was buried on 3 Apr 1858 in West Tisted, Hampshire, England.[141]

Noted events in her life were:
• Resided: on a stock farm, 1841, West Tisted, Hampshire, England. [3]

• Resided: 1851, West Tisted, Hampshire, England. [4]

Hannah married **William Paice**[15] on 22 Oct 1804 in Froxfield, Hampshire, England. [16]

24. George Kerr was born about 1780. Other names for George were George Carr and George Keer.

Research Notes:
Many Kerrs came to Ulster province in northern Ireland during the Scottish plantation in the 1700s. Irish lands were taken from Catholics and given to Protestants arriving from Great Britain.

George Kerr lived in the post-town of Carrick, which lies between Carrick Lough (lake) and the market town of Derrygonnelly in the County Fermanagh in Ulster. Both towns are just south of the Lower Lough Erne. Carrick is 129 arcres of rolling pasture in the Inishmacsaint parish. The ruins of a 15th century church, Teampall Carraig, and Castle Tully are nearby. The castle was built for Sir John Hume, a Scottish planter, in 1619 and occupied until 1641 when it was sacked.

George Kerr's children were born in Carrick. When George's son George moved a mile south to Derrygonnelly, there were five homes in Carrick, four of which were occupied by Kerrs. In the 1700s Carrick was called Mullaghanelly, an Irish word meaning Poet Hill.

George Kerr, perhaps the grandfather of George Kerr, paid rent for land in Mullaghanelly in 1742 according to the "Rent roll of the mannor [sic] of castle Hume and Tully."

Gabriel Kerr and George Kerr of Mullaghanelly were listed as landholders in July 1751 in the "Freeholders List of Electors for Fermanagh 1747-1768,"

Gabriel Kerr of Mullaghanelly paid rent in 1793, according to the "Earl of Ely Rent Rolls for 1793," to the Manor of Tully.

Hume and Tully manor was built in 1728, but by 1793 it was in ruin. What remains is an octagonal dovecote (pigeon shelter) and the L-shaped stables and courtyard, which are located near the present-day Lough Erne Golf Resort.

Noted events in his life were:
• Land: freeholder, 1801, Drumcroohan, Fermanagh, Ireland. [188]

• Resided: 1806, Carrick, Fermanagh, Ireland. [91]

• Resided: 1836, Carrick, Fermanagh, Ireland. [189]

George married **Margaret Eaton** about 1805 in Ireland.

Children from this marriage were:

    i.   **Elizabeth Kerr** was born in Carrick, Fermanagh, Ireland[91] and was baptized on 13 Jul 1806 in Upper Inishmacsaint, Fermanagh, Ireland.[91]

    ii.   **John Kerr** was born in Carrick, Fermanagh, Ireland[91] and was baptized on 30 Apr 1808 in Upper Inishmacsaint, Fermanagh, Ireland.[91]

    iii.   **Jane Kerr** was born in Carrick, Fermanagh, Ireland and was baptized on 13 May 1810 in Upper Inishmacsaint, Fermanagh, Ireland.[91]

    iv.   **Jane Kerr** was born in Carrick, Fermanagh, Ireland[91] and was baptized on 11 Oct 1811 in Fermanagh, Ireland.[91]

12   v.   **George Kerr**[14]

25. Margaret Eaton.

Margaret married **George Kerr** about 1805 in Ireland.

Sixth Generation (3rd Great-Grandparents)

32. Samuel Heasman, son of **William Heasman** and **Rachel Medhurst,** was baptized on 12 Jan 1736 in Saint Swithuns, East Grinstead, Sussex, England[6] and was buried on 24 Oct 1815 in East Grinstead, Sussex, England.[119]

Samuel married **Sarah Wheatley** on 7 Apr 1760 in Saint Swithuns, East Grinstead, Sussex, England.[120]

Children from this marriage were:

	i.	**John Heasman** was baptized on 30 Jan 1761 in East Grinstead, Sussex, England.[190]
	ii.	**Samuel Heasman** was baptized on 10 Oct 1762 in East Grinstead, Sussex, England.[82]
	iii.	**Sarah Heasman** was baptized on 1 Jan 1765 in East Grinstead, Sussex, England. [82]
	iv.	**Edward Wheatley Heasman** was baptized on 17 Feb 1768 in East Grinstead, Sussex, England.[82]
	v.	**Anna Heasman** was baptized on 25 Jul 1770 in East Grinstead, Sussex, England.[82]
	vi.	**William Heasman** was baptized on 24 Feb 1773 in East Grinstead, Sussex, England[10] and was buried on 16 Feb 1855 in Hartfield, Sussex, England.[5]
16	vii.	**James Heasman**
	viii.	**Susanna Heasman** was baptized on 2 Feb 1785 in East Grinstead, Sussex, England.[82]

33. Sarah Wheatley, daughter of **Edward Wheatley** and **Anne Vinall,** was baptized on 18 Feb 1740 in Saint Margarets Church, West Hoathly, Sussex, England[5] and was buried on 3 Feb 1806 in Saint Swithuns, East Grinstead, Sussex, England.[2]

Sarah married **Samuel Heasman** on 7 Apr 1760 in Saint Swithuns, East Grinstead, Sussex, England.[120]

34. Thomas Turk, son of **John Turk** and **Sarah Brown,** was baptized on 17 Feb 1745 in Saint Denys, Rotherfield, Sussex, England[10] and was buried on 5 Jul 1832 in Saint Mary the Virgin Church, Hartfield, Sussex, England.[5]

General Notes: He was a farmer.

Thomas married **Mary**.

Children from this marriage were:

i.	**Jane Turk** was baptized on 31 Jul 1768 in Saint Peters Church, Pembury, Kent, England.[10]
ii.	**Thomas Turk** was baptized on 3 Sep 1769 in Saint Peters Church, Pembury, Kent, England.[1]
iii.	**Sarah Turk** was baptized on 21 Oct 1770 in Saint Peters Church, Pembury, Kent, England.[1]
iv.	**Anne Turk** was baptized on 10 May 1772 in Saint Peters Church, Pembury, Kent, England.[6]
v.	**John Turk** was baptized on 20 Mar 1774 in Saint Peters Church, Pembury, Kent, England[10] and died circa Apr 1847 in Sussex, England[191] about age 73.
vi.	**Mary Turk** was baptized on 9 Apr 1775 in Saint Peters Church, Pembury, Kent,

England.[6]

   17   vii.   **Elizabeth Turk**

Thomas next married **Ann Harrard** on 21 Oct 1809 in Saint Bartholomews Church, Maresfield, Sussex, England.[155]

35. Mary was born circa 1745 and was buried on 13 Jul 1808 in Hartfield, Sussex, England. [5]

Mary married **Thomas Turk.**

36. John Shoebridge,[7] son of **John Shewbridge** and **Mary Pollard,** was baptized on 31 Dec 1723 in Saint Mary the Virgin Church, Hartfield, Sussex, England[10] and was buried on 20 Dec 1794 in Saint Mary the Virgin Church, Hartfield, Sussex, England. [125]

John married **Elizabeth Wood**[131] on 8 May 1760 in Hartfield, Sussex, England. [15]

Children from this marriage were:

        i.   **Philadelphia Shoebridge** was baptized on 26 Nov 1764 in Hartfield, Sussex, England[7] and was buried on 16 Apr 1766 in Saint Mary the Virgin Church, Hartfield, Sussex, England.[187]
        ii.   **Anna Shoebridge** was baptized on 19 Jun 1767 in Hartfield, Sussex, England. [7]
        iii.   **Letitia "Letty" Shoebridge** was baptized on 28 Apr 1771 in Hartfield, Sussex, England[7] and died circa Nov 1851 in Sussex, England[8] about age 80.
        iv.   **John Shoebridge** was baptized on 31 Oct 1773 in Hartfield, Sussex, England. [7]
   18   v.   **Jesse Shoebridge**[6]

37. Elizabeth Wood,[131] daughter of **Thomas Wood**[10] and **Ann Butching,**[10] was baptized on 23 Mar 1739 in East Grinstead, Sussex, England[10] and was buried on 9 Dec 1813 in Hartfield, Sussex, England.[125]

Elizabeth married **John Shoebridge**[7] on 8 May 1760 in Hartfield, Sussex, England. [15]

38. William Weller,[1] son of **George Weller**[10] and **Mary,**[10] was baptized on 31 Aug 1726 in Speldhurst, Kent, England[10] and was buried on 4 Apr 1777 in Speldhurst, Kent, England. [125]

William married **Sarah Andrews** on 10 Oct 1751 in Saint Lawrence Church, Bidborough, Kent, England.[15]

Children from this marriage were:

        i.   **William Weller** was born on 21 Oct 1752,[1] was baptized on 5 Nov 1752 in Ashurst, Kent, England,[1] and died circa Aug 1838 in Kent, England[8] about age 85.
        ii.   **Henry Weller** was born on 6 Jan 1755 and was baptized on 19 Jan 1755 in Ashurst, Kent, England.[1]
        iii.   **Sarah Weller** was baptized on 15 Jan 1758 in Ashurst, Kent, England. [1]
        iv.   **Hannah Weller** was born on 1 Dec 1759[1] and was baptized on 23 Dec 1759 in Ashurst, Kent, England.[1]
        v.   **Mary Weller** was born on 16 Mar 1762[1] and was baptized on 18 Apr 1762 in Ashurst, Kent, England.[1]
   19   vi.   **Karen "Carey" Weller**

39. Sarah Andrews, daughter of **Benjamin Andrews,** was baptized on 6 Dec 1732 in Ashurst, Kent, England[10] and was buried on 20 Apr 1791 in Speldhurst, Kent, England. [125]

Sarah married **William Weller**[1] on 10 Oct 1751 in Saint Lawrence Church, Bidborough, Kent, England.[15]

40. John Stubbs, son of **William Stubbs,** was baptized on 29 Apr 1739 in East Meon, Hampshire, England[133] and was buried on 17 May 1824 in Ropley, Hampshire, England.[2]

> Noted events in his life were:
> • Occupation: husbandman, 1763, East Meon, Hampshire, England.[192]

John married **Ann Chace,** daughter of **Robert Chace,** on 27 Nov 1763 in East Meon, Hampshire, England.[193]

Children from this marriage were:

> i.   **Mary Stubbs** was baptized on 12 Jun 1764 in East Meon, Hampshire, England[194] and was buried on 6 Sep 1764 in East Meon, Hampshire, England.[194]
> ii.   **John Stubbs** was baptized on 20 Apr 1766 in East Meon, Hampshire, England.[194]
> iii.   **Ann Stubbs** was baptized on 24 May 1767 in East Meon, Hampshire, England.[196]

John next married **Elizabeth Budd** on 31 Oct 1774 in Ropley, Hampshire, England.[15]

Children from this marriage were:

> i.   **William Stubbs** was born in 1775 in Ropley, Hampshire, England[197] and was baptized on 2 Apr 1775 in Ropley, Hampshire, England.[197]
> ii.   **Thomas Stubbs** was born in 1777 in Ropley, Hampshire, England.[197]
> iii.   **Henry Stubbs** was born circa 1778 in Ropley, Hampshire, England,[198] died on 11 Oct 1870 in Woodlands, West Meon, Hampshire, England[199] about age 92, and was buried on 17 Oct 1870 in Ropley, Hampshire, England.[200]
> 20   iv.   **James Stubbs**[12]
> v.   **Elizabeth Stubbs** was baptized on 16 May 1785 in Ropley, Hampshire, England[201] and died circa Feb 1866 in Hampshire, England[8] about age 80.
> vi.   **Michael Stubbs** was born on 25 Mar 1787 in Ropley, Hampshire, England,[7] was baptized on 22 Apr 1787 in Ropley, Hampshire, England,[7] died on 24 Jul 1859 in Froxfield, Hampshire, England[202] at age 72, and was buried on 29 Jul 1859 in Froxfield, Hampshire, England.[7]
> vii.   **Jane Stubbs** was born on 19 Nov 1789 in Ropley, Hampshire, England,[7] was baptized on 13 Dec 1789 in Ropley, Hampshire, England,[7] and was buried on 12 Sep 1790 in Ropley, Hampshire, England.[7]

41. Elizabeth Budd, daughter of **John Budd**[136] and **Elizabeth Stephens,** was baptized on 18 Apr 1754 in All Saints Church, Steep, Hampshire, England[134] and died circa Oct 1849 in Ropley, Hampshire, England[132] about age 95.

> General Notes: Elizabeth Budd lived to be quite old and in the Ropley register it is written: "Elizabeth Stubbs died aged 95 and a half years old and while living made 5 generations all alive and left about 120 living branches of which she had been the root." There is a small gravestone to her in Ropley Churchyard.[203]

Elizabeth married **John Stubbs** on 31 Oct 1774 in Ropley, Hampshire, England.[15]

42. Richard Wateridge was born about 1760 and was buried on 21 Sep 1824 in Medstead, Hampshire, England.[125]

Richard married **Elizabeth Pink** on 11 May 1781 in Old Alresford, Hampshire, England.[12]

Children from this marriage were:

i. **Ann Wateridge** was baptized on 27 Oct 1781 in Medstead, Hampshire, England.[10]
21 ii. **Mary Wateridge**
iii. **Elizabeth "Betty" Wateridge** was baptized on 1 Apr 1787 in Medstead, Hampshire, England[10] and died in Jul 1860 in Alresford, Hampshire, England[8] at age 73.
iv. **John Wateridge** was baptized on 4 Jul 1790 in Medstead, Hampshire, England.[10]
v. **Jane Wateridge** was baptized on 29 Mar 1795 in Medstead, Hampshire, England.[10]

43. Elizabeth Pink, daughter of **John Pink**[139] and **Elizabeth,**[139] was baptized on 8 Oct 1760 in Bishops Waltham, Hampshire, England[135] and was buried on 27 Jan 1826 in Medstead, Hampshire, England.[125]

Elizabeth married **Richard Wateridge** on 11 May 1781 in Old Alresford, Hampshire, England.[12]

47. Mary Aldred[6] was baptized on 2 Jun 1759 in Steep, Hampshire, England.

Mary had a child.

Her child was:

23 i. **Hannah Aldred**

Mary married **Thomas Wiggins** on 12 Apr 1789 in Steep, Hampshire, England.[137]

Seventh Generation (4th Great-Grandparents)

64. William Heasman, son of **Edward Heasman** and **Jane,** was baptized on 18 Oct 1689 in Saint Swithuns, East Grinstead, Sussex, England[6] and was buried on 8 Apr 1772 in Saint Swithuns, East Grinstead, Sussex, England.[2]

William married **Rachel Medhurst** on 23 Dec 1720 in Saint Thomas à Becket Church, Framfield, Sussex, England.[16]

Children from this marriage were:

      i.   **William Heasman** was baptized on 3 Oct 1721 in Saint Swithuns, East Grinstead, Sussex, England.[155]

      ii.   **John Heasman** was baptized on 10 Dec 1723 in Saint Swithuns, East Grinstead, Sussex, England.[155]

      iii.   **Robert Heasman** was baptized on 19 Jan 1724 in Saint Swithuns, East Grinstead, Sussex, England[155] and died on 24 Aug 1789 in East Grinstead, Sussex, England at age 65.

      iv.   **Edward Heasman** was baptized on 8 Sep 1727 in Saint Swithuns, East Grinstead, Sussex, England.[155]

      v.   **Thomas Heasman** was baptized on 5 May 1730 in Saint Swithuns, East Grinstead, Sussex, England.[155]

      vi.   **James Heasman** was baptized on 17 Apr 1732 in Saint Swithuns, East Grinstead, Sussex, England.[155]

      vii.   **Henry Heasman** was baptized on 3 Mar 1733 in Saint Swithuns, East Grinstead, Sussex, England.[155]

  32 viii.   **Samuel Heasman**

      ix.   **Elizabeth Heasman** was baptized on 11 Apr 1742 in Saint Swithuns, East Grinstead, Sussex, England.[155]

      x.   **Elizabeth Heasman** was baptized on 8 Mar 1748 in East Grinstead, Sussex, England.[6]

65. Rachel Medhurst, daughter of **William Medhurst**[150] and **Elizabeth Cornwell,** was baptized on 2 Feb 1702 in Saint Thomas à Becket Church, Framfield, Sussex, England[6] and was buried on 29 Jan 1775 in Saint Swithuns, East Grinstead, Sussex, England.[2]

Rachel married **William Heasman** on 23 Dec 1720 in Saint Thomas à Becket Church, Framfield, Sussex, England.[16]

66. Edward Wheatley, son of **Edward Wheatley**[155] and **Timothea "Timothy" Mills,**[155] was baptized on 25 Mar 1692 in West Hoathly, Sussex, England[121] and was buried on 18 Jan 1768 in Saint Bartholomews Church, Maresfield, Sussex, England.[122]

    Noted events in his life were:
    • Occupation: weaver.[155]

Edward married **Anne Vinall** on 2 Feb 1724 in Saint Swithuns, East Grinstead, Sussex, England.[123]

Children from this marriage were:

      i.   **John Wheatley** was baptized on 20 Jan 1725 in Saint Margarets Church, West Hoathly, Sussex, England[204] and was buried on 23 Apr 1797 in Saint Bartholomews Church, Maresfield, Sussex, England.[155]

      ii.   **Anne Wheatley**[155] was baptized on 8 Nov 1728 in Saint Margarets Church, West

Hoathly, Sussex, England[5] and died in May 1805[155] at age 76.

    iii.   **William Wheatley** was baptized on 2 Oct 1730 in Saint Margarets Church, West Hoathly, Sussex, England[5] and was buried on 7 Mar 1810 in Saint Margaret the Queen Church, Buxted, Sussex, England.[155]

    iv.   **Mary Wheatley**[155] was baptized on 16 Jul 1732 in Saint Margarets Church, West Hoathly, Sussex, England.[5]

    v.   **Edward Wheatley**[155] was baptized on 23 Aug 1734 in Saint Margarets Church, West Hoathly, Sussex, England[5] and was buried on 20 Sep 1734 in West Hoathly, Sussex, England.[155]

    vi.   **Elizabeth Wheatley**[155] was baptized on 1 Dec 1738 in Saint Margarets Church, West Hoathly, Sussex, England.[5]

33   vii.   **Sarah Wheatley**

67. Anne Vinall was buried on 20 Jul 1783 in Saint Bartholomews Church, Maresfield, Sussex, England.[124]

> Research Notes: Vinall is a common name in the area, and her father may have been Thomas from Lindfield or Ellis from Wivelsfield.

Anne married **Edward Wheatley** on 2 Feb 1724 in Saint Swithuns, East Grinstead, Sussex, England.[123]

68. John Turk, son of **John Turk** and **Sarah Browne,** was baptized on 5 Mar 1712 in Saint Denys, Rotherfield, Sussex, England[10] and was buried on 15 Jan 1787 in Saint Denys, Rotherfield, Sussex, England.[125]

Noted events in his life were:
• Occupation: farmer, 1740, Rotherfield, Sussex, England.[126]

John married **Sarah Brown** on 5 Aug 1740 in Fleet Prison, Central London, London, England.[126]

> Marriage Notes: Fleet Prison was a historic London prison, dating back at least to William the Conqueror and Norman days. It was named after the Fleet stream, a tributary of the Thames. "Fleet" marriages were performed near Fleet prison, and people who could not obtain a marriage license went to Fleet Prison to receive a street-side, no-questions-asked marriage. John and Sarah probably could not secure a license because they were first cousins. They married a few months after John Turk's father's death.

Children from this marriage were:

    i.   **Sarah Turk** was baptized on 8 Dec 1741 in Saint Denys, Rotherfield, Sussex, England.[10]

    ii.   **Mary Turk** was baptized on 4 May 1743 in Saint Denys, Rotherfield, Sussex, England.[10]

    iii.   **John Turk** was baptized on 4 Aug 1744 in Saint Denys, Rotherfield, Sussex, England.[10]

34   iv.   **Thomas Turk**

    v.   **Anne Turk** was baptized on 15 Oct 1747 in Saint Denys, Rotherfield, Sussex, England[10] and was buried on 2 Mar 1824 in Saint Denys, Rotherfield, Sussex, England.[5]

    vi.   **Richard Turk** was baptized on 12 Feb 1748 in Saint Denys, Rotherfield, Sussex, England.[10]

    vii.   **Joseph Turk** was baptized on 17 Mar 1750 in Saint Denys, Rotherfield, Sussex, England[10] and was buried on 5 Mar 1824 in Saint Denys, Rotherfield, Sussex, England.[125]

viii.   **Elizabeth Turk** was baptized on 1 Oct 1752 in Saint Denys, Rotherfield, Sussex, England[10] and was buried on 25 Apr 1754 in Saint Denys, Rotherfield, Sussex, England.[125]

ix.   **Jane Turk** was baptized on 10 Mar 1754 in Saint Denys, Rotherfield, Sussex, England[10] and was buried on 29 Mar 1754 in Saint Denys, Rotherfield, Sussex, England.[125]

x.   **Benjamin Turk** was baptized on 31 Aug 1755 in Saint Denys, Rotherfield, Sussex, England[10] and was buried on 13 Nov 1757 in Saint Denys, Rotherfield, Sussex, England.[125]

xi.   **Hannah Turk** was baptized on 12 Aug 1759 in Saint Denys, Rotherfield, Sussex, England[10] and was buried on 10 Apr 1836 in Saint Denys, Rotherfield, Sussex, England.[5]

xii.   **Lucy Turk** was baptized on 1 Nov 1761 in Saint Denys, Rotherfield, Sussex, England[10] and died in May 1852 in Rotherfield, Sussex, England[8] at age 90.

69. Sarah Brown, daughter of **William Browne** and **Sarah Bridger,** was baptized on 8 Mar 1717 in Saint Michaels Church, Withyham, Sussex, England[10] and was buried on 25 Jan 1793 in Saint Denys, Rotherfield, Sussex, England.[125]

Sarah married **John Turk** on 5 Aug 1740 in Fleet Prison, Central London, London, England.[126]

72. John Shewbridge, son of **John Shewbridge** and **Mary Pope,** was baptized on 31 Jul 1698 in Saint Mary the Virgin Church, Hartfield, Sussex, England[1] and was buried on 28 Dec 1770 in Saint Mary the Virgin Church, Hartfield, Sussex, England.[125] Another name for John was John Shoebridge.

John married **Mary Pollard** on 19 Feb 1723 in Saint Mary the Virgin Church, Hartfield, Sussex, England.[12]

Children from this marriage were:

36   i.   **John Shoebridge**[7]

     ii.   **Mary Shoebridge** was baptized on 21 Nov 1725 in Hartfield, Sussex, England.

    iii.   **Sarah Shoebridge** was baptized on 12 Feb 1727 in Hartfield, Sussex, England.[10]

    iv.   **Elizabeth Shoebridge** was baptized on 15 Nov 1730 in Hartfield, Sussex, England.[5]

     v.   **Samuel Shoebridge** was baptized on 11 Apr 1736 in Hartfield, Sussex, England.[1]

    vi.   **William Shoebridge** was baptized on 21 Oct 1738 in Hartfield, Sussex, England.[1]

73. Mary Pollard, daughter of **John Pollard,** was baptized on 15 Jun 1699 in Hartfield, Sussex, England.[1]

Mary married **John Shewbridge** on 19 Feb 1723 in Saint Mary the Virgin Church, Hartfield, Sussex, England.[12]

74. Thomas Wood,[10] son of **Thomas Wood** and **Mary Marchant,**[10] was baptized on 7 Jun 1705 in East Grinstead, Sussex, England[10] and was buried on 21 Dec 1761 in East Grinstead, Sussex, England.[5]

Thomas married **Ann Butching**[10] on 4 Apr 1733 in East Grinstead, Sussex, England.[12]

Children from this marriage were:

     i.   **Thomas Wood** was baptized on 7 Apr 1734 in East Grinstead, Sussex, England[6] and was buried on 11 Nov 1809 in East Grinstead, Sussex, England. [125]

    ii.   **Mary Wood**[10] was baptized on 20 Aug 1734 in East Grinstead, Sussex, England.

    iii.   **Ann Wood** was baptized on 5 May 1736 in East Grinstead, Sussex, England. [6]

37   iv.   **Elizabeth Wood**[131]

75. Ann Butching,[10] daughter of **William Butching**[10] and **Elizabeth,**[10] was baptized on 2 Feb 1703 in East Grinstead, Sussex, England[10] and was buried on 22 Jan 1780 in East Grinstead, Sussex, England. [125]

Ann married **Thomas Wood**[10] on 4 Apr 1733 in East Grinstead, Sussex, England. [12]

76. George Weller[10] was baptized circa 1700.

George married **Mary**.[10]

Children from this marriage were:

    i.   **George Weller** was baptized on 29 Aug 1721 in Speldhurst, Kent, England. [10]

38   ii.   **William Weller**[1]

77. Mary.[10]

Mary married **George Weller**.[10]

78. Benjamin Andrews.[10]

Benjamin married someone.

His children were:

39   i.   **Sarah Andrews**

    ii.   **Mary Andrews** was baptized on 16 Feb 1734 in Ashurst, Kent, England. [1]

80. William Stubbs[10] was born circa 1710.

William married someone.

His children were:

    i.   **Jane Stubbs** was baptized on 24 Aug 1735 in East Meon, Hampshire, England. [10]

40   ii.   **John Stubbs**

82. John Budd,[136] son of **Giles Budd** and **Frances Smith,** was baptized on 13 Dec 1727 in All Saints Church, Steep, Hampshire, England[137] and was buried on 20 May 1770 in Steep, Hampshire, England.[137]

John married **Elizabeth Stephens** on 26 Apr 1753 in All Saints Church, Steep, Hampshire, England.[137]

Children from this marriage were:

41   i.   **Elizabeth Budd**

    ii.   **Ann Budd** was baptized in Mar 1756 in Steep, Hampshire, England. [137]

    iii.   **John Budd** was baptized on 12 Jan 1758 in Steep, Hampshire, England. [137]

    iv.   **Thomas Budd** was baptized on 18 Jul 1760 in Steep, Hampshire, England[205] and was buried on 1 Dec 1851 in Steep, Hampshire, England. [137]

v.	**William Budd** was baptized 12 Aprl 1762 in Steep, Hampshire, England. [137]
vi.	**Mary Budd** was baptized on 20 May 1764 in Steep, Hampshire, England. [137]
vii.	**Sarah Budd** was baptized on 1 Apr 1770 in Steep, Hampshire, England. [137]

83. Elizabeth Stephens, daughter of **Thomas Stephens,** was baptized on 31 May 1732 in East Meon, Hampshire, England[138] and was buried on 21 Mar 1805 in Steep, Hampshire, England. [137]

Elizabeth married **John Budd**[136] on 26 Apr 1753 in All Saints Church, Steep, Hampshire, England.[137]

86. John Pink[139] was born about 1730.

John married **Elizabeth**.[139]

The child from this marriage was:

    43   i.   **Elizabeth Pink**

87. Elizabeth.[139]

Elizabeth married **John Pink**.[139]

Ancestor Report for Frederick Keith Heasman

Eighth Generation (5th Great-Grandparents)

128. Edward Heasman, son of **John Heasman** and **Ann Bane,** was baptized on 2 Feb 1666 in Saint Swithuns, East Grinstead, Sussex, England[6] and was buried on 11 Dec 1737 in Saint Swithuns, East Grinstead, Sussex, England.[2]

Edward married **Jane** circa 1688.

Children from this marriage were:

    64   i.   **William Heasman**
          ii. **John Heasman** was baptized on 20 Nov 1691 in Saint Swithuns, East Grinstead, Sussex, England.[10]
        iii. **Robert Heasman** was baptized on 27 Mar 1695 in Saint Swithuns, East Grinstead, Sussex, England.[10]
        iv. **Elizabeth Heasman** was baptized on 24 Oct 1704 in Saint Swithuns, East Grinstead, Sussex, England.[10]
         v. **Edward Heasman** was baptized on 27 Mar 1706 in Saint Swithuns, East Grinstead, Sussex, England[5] and was buried on 23 Jun 1762 in East Grinstead, Sussex, England.[125]

129. Jane was born circa 1669 and was buried on 2 Nov 1730 in Saint Swithuns, East Grinstead, Sussex, England.[2]

Jane married **Edward Heasman** circa 1688.

130. William Medhurst,[150] son of **William Medhurst** and **Sarah,**[150] was baptized on 9 May 1667 in Saint Mary the Virgin Church, Hartfield, Sussex, England[6] and was buried on 29 Apr 1740 in Saint Thomas à Becket Church, Framfield, Sussex, England.[2]

    Birth Notes: In the Bishop's transcription of the baptism, his mother is listed as Elizabeth but I believe it a mistranscription. He is listed in his sister's will and her mother is Sarah.

    General Notes: He worked as a pail maker in Framfield.

William married **Elizabeth Cornwell** on 14 Apr 1691 in Saint Mary the Virgin Church, Ringmer, Sussex, England.[16]

Children from this marriage were:

          i. **William Medhurst** was baptized on 22 May 1691 in Framfield, Sussex, England.[6]
         ii. **Mary Medhurst** was baptized on 8 Jun 1692 in Framfield, Sussex, England.[6]
        iii. **Edward Medhurst** was baptized on 20 Sep 1695 in Framfield, Sussex, England.[6]
        iv. **George Medhurst** was baptized on 22 Jan 1697 in Framfield, Sussex, England.[6]
         v. **Lucy Medhurst** was baptized on 31 Jul 1700 in Framfield, Sussex, England.[6]
    65 vi. **Rachel Medhurst**
       vii. **Anne Medhurst** was baptized on 15 Dec 1708 in Framfield, Sussex, England.[5]
     viii. **Elizabeth Medhurst** was baptized on 27 Dec 1708 in Framfield, Sussex, England.[5]

131. Elizabeth Cornwell, daughter of **George Cornwell Jr.**[151] and **Mary,** was baptized on 18 Feb 1665 in Saint Denys, Rotherfield, Sussex, England.[10]

Elizabeth married **William Medhurst**[150] on 14 Apr 1691 in Saint Mary the Virgin Church, Ringmer, Sussex, England.[16]

132. Edward Wheatley,[155] son of **William Wheatley** and **Ann Kidder**,[155] was baptized on 25 Mar 1656 in Ringmer, Sussex, England[155] and was buried on 17 May 1727 in West Hoathly, Sussex, England.[155]

Noted events in his life were:
• Occupation: weaver.[155]

• Will:

Edward married **Timothea "Timothy" Mills**[155] on 3 Aug 1688 in West Hoathly, Sussex, England.

Children from this marriage were:

  i. **Anne Wheatley**[155] was baptized on 19 May 1689 in West Hoathly, Sussex, England.[155]

  ii. **Mary Wheatley**[155] was baptized on 28 Nov 1690 in West Hoathly, Sussex, England[155] and was buried on 9 May 1775 in Ardingly Parish Church, Ardingly, , Sussex, England.[155]

66 iii. **Edward Wheatley**

  iv. **Elizabeth Wheatley**[155] was baptized on 17 Nov 1693 in West Hoathly, Sussex, England[155] and was buried on 2 Feb 1762 in West Hoathly, Sussex, England.[155]

  v. **William Wheatley**[155] was baptized on 31 May 1695 in West Hoathly, Sussex, England[155] and was buried on 14 Jun 1695 in West Hoathly, Sussex, England.[155]

  vi. **Sarah Wheatley**[155] was baptized on 18 Jul 1696 in West Hoathly, Sussex, England[155] and was buried on 14 Mar 1696 in West Hoathly, Sussex, England.[155]

  vii. **Jane Wheatley**[155] was baptized on 18 May 1698 in West Hoathly, Sussex, England[155] and was buried on 31 Jan 1767 in West Hoathly, Sussex, England.[155]

  viii. **John Wheatley**[155] was born in 1699 in Bolney, , Sussex, England[155] and was baptized on 26 Dec 1699 in West Hoathly, Sussex, England.[155]

  ix. **Sarah Wheatley**[155] was baptized on 31 Aug 1702 in West Hoathly, Sussex, England.[155]

  x. **Timothea Wheatley**[155] was baptized on 11 Apr 1704 in West Hoathly, Sussex, England[155] and was buried on 24 Oct 1762 in Ardingly Parish Church, Ardingly, , Sussex, England.[155]

  xi. **Ambrose Wheatley**[155] was baptized on 29 Mar 1711 in West Hoathly, Sussex, England[155] and was buried in 1765.[155]

133. Timothea "Timothy" Mills[155] was born circa 1665[155] and was buried on 6 Feb 1751 in West Hoathly, Sussex, England.[155]

Timothea married **Edward Wheatley**[155] on 3 Aug 1688 in West Hoathly, Sussex, England.

136. John Turk, son of **John Turk** and **Mary,** was baptized on 3 Jul 1681 in Saint Denys, Rotherfield, Sussex, England[10] and was buried on 5 Apr 1740 in Saint Denys, Rotherfield, Sussex, England.[125]

Noted events in his life were:
• Resided: 1715, Rotherfield, Sussex, England.[206]

John married **Sarah Browne** on 23 Oct 1705 in All Saints Church, Lewes, Sussex, England.[16]

Children from this marriage were:

  i. **Mary Turk** was baptized on 24 Nov 1706 in Saint Denys, Rotherfield, Sussex,

England[10] and was buried on 15 Jan 1779 in Pembury, Kent, England.[2]

    68   ii.   **John Turk**

         iii.   **William Turk** was baptized on 6 Jan 1715 in Saint Denys, Rotherfield, Sussex, England[207] and was buried on 1 Mar 1795 in Saint Denys, Rotherfield, Sussex, England.[208]

137. Sarah Browne, daughter of **William Browne**[159] and **Katherine Longly,** was baptized on 25 May 1675 in Saint Michaels Church, Withyham, Sussex, England[10] and was buried on 12 Feb 1758 in Saint Denys, Rotherfield, Sussex, England.[125]

Sarah married **John Turk** on 23 Oct 1705 in All Saints Church, Lewes, Sussex, England.[16]

138. William Browne, son of **William Browne**[159] and **Katherine Longly,** was baptized on 17 Mar 1681 in Saint Michaels Church, Withyham, Sussex, England[10] and was buried on 17 May 1729 in Saint Michaels Church, Withyham, Sussex, England.[160]

William married **Sarah Bridger** on 11 Sep 1711 in Saint Michaels Church, Withyham, Sussex, England.[12]

Children from this marriage were:

         i.   **John Browne** was baptized on 29 Sep 1714 in Withyham, Sussex, England.[10]

    69   ii.   **Sarah Brown**

         iii.   **Mary Browne** was baptized on 30 Sep 1720 in Withyham, Sussex, England.[10]

139. Sarah Bridger, daughter of **John Bridger** and **Sarah Coe,** was baptized on 19 Oct 1690 in Saint Denys, Rotherfield, Sussex, England[10] and was buried on 15 Apr 1728 in Saint Michaels Church, Withyham, Sussex, England.[160]

Sarah married **William Browne** on 11 Sep 1711 in Saint Michaels Church, Withyham, Sussex, England.[12]

144. John Shewbridge was born in 1676[163] and was buried on 15 Jul 1755 in Saint Mary the Virgin Church, Hartfield, Sussex, England.[125]

John married **Mary Pope** on 27 Mar 1698 in Saint Peter and Saint Paul, Wadhurst, Sussex, England.[16]

Children from this marriage were:

    72   i.   **John Shewbridge**

         ii.   **Elizabeth Shewbridge** was baptized in Nov 1700 in Saint Mary the Virgin Church, Hartfield, Sussex, England.[5]

         iii.   **Richard Shewbridge** was baptized on 9 Aug 1702 in Hartfield, Sussex, England[10] and was buried on 4 Feb 1779 in Hartfield, Sussex, England.[5]

         iv.   **Mary Shewbridge** was baptized on 22 Sep 1704 in Hartfield, Sussex, England[5] and was buried on 4 Oct 1785 in Hartfield, Sussex, England.[5]

         v.   **Sarah Shewbridge** was baptized on 6 Sep 1706 in Saint Mary the Virgin Church, Hartfield, Sussex, England.[10]

         vi.   **Thomas Shewbridge** was baptized on 29 Jun 1708 in Hartfield, Sussex, England[6] and was buried on 24 Dec 1773 in Hartfield, Sussex, England.[125]

         vii.   **William Shewbridge** was baptized on 14 May 1710 in Hartfield, Sussex, England.[10]

         viii.   **Robert Shewbridge** was baptized on 1 Oct 1712 in Hartfield, Sussex, England[10] and was buried on 4 Oct 1712 in Hartfield, Sussex, England.[125]

145. Mary Pope, daughter of **Robart Pope** and **Ann Plano,** was born in 1672,[163] was baptized on 11 Aug 1672 in Hartfield, Sussex, England,[6] and was buried on 8 Nov 1759 in Saint Mary the Virgin Church, Hartfield, Sussex, England.[5]

Mary married **John Shewbridge** on 27 Mar 1698 in Saint Peter and Saint Paul, Wadhurst, Sussex, England.[16]

146. John Pollard[1] was born about 1675.

John married someone.

His child was:

    73   i.   **Mary Pollard**

148. Thomas Wood, son of **Thomas Wood** and **Elizabeth Croft,** was baptized on 15 Feb 1670 in East Grinstead, Sussex, England.[10]

Thomas married **Mary Marchant**[10] on 23 May 1704 in East Grinstead, Sussex, England.[12]

Children from this marriage were:

    74   i.   **Thomas Wood**[10]
          ii.   **Henry Wood** was baptized on 25 Nov 1709 in East Grinstead, Sussex, England.[10]

149. Mary Marchant,[10] daughter of **Arthur Marchant** and **Mary Winder,** was baptized on 26 Sep 1675 in Rotherfield, Sussex, England.[1]

Mary married **Thomas Wood** on 23 May 1704 in East Grinstead, Sussex, England.[12]

150. William Butching.[10]

William married **Elizabeth.**[10]

The child from this marriage was:

    75   i.   **Ann Butching**[10]

151. Elizabeth.[10]

    Research Notes: Some researchers think Elizabeth's surname is Winne. This is plausible but not proven.

Elizabeth married **William Butching.**[10]

164. Giles Budd was born about 1695.

Giles married **Frances Smith** on 13 Jan 1715 in Steep, Hampshire, England.[137]

Children from this marriage were:

          i.   **Frances Budd** was baptized on 12 May 1716 in Steep, Hampshire, England.[137]
          ii.   **Mary Budd** was baptized on 17 Jan 1720 in Steep, Hampshire, England.[137]
          iii.   **Giles Budd** was baptized on 14 Mar 1722 in Steep, Hampshire, England.[137]
    82   iv.   **John Budd**[136]

165. Frances Smith, daughter of **William Smith,** was born about 1695 and was buried on 18 Sep 1764 in Steep, Hampshire, England.[137]

Frances married **Giles Budd** on 13 Jan 1715 in Steep, Hampshire, England.[137]

166. Thomas Stephens[6] was born circa 1700.

Thomas married someone.

His children were:

83	i.	**Elizabeth Stephens**
	ii.	**Thomas Stephens** was baptized on 5 Nov 1734 in East Meon, Hampshire, England.[164]

Ancestor Report for Frederick Keith Heasman

Ancestor Report for Frederick Keith Heasman

Ninth Generation (6th Great-Grandparents)

256. John Heasman, son of **Francis Heasman** and **Bridget Foord,** was baptized on 19 Jan 1621 in Saint Swithuns, East Grinstead, Sussex, England[142] and was buried on 11 Nov 1698 in Saint Swithuns, East Grinstead, Sussex, England. [143]

John married **Susan Heritage** on 10 Sep 1644 in Saint Swithuns, East Grinstead, Sussex, England.[209]

Children from this marriage were:

       i.   **Henry Heasman** was baptized on 20 Jul 1645 in East Grinstead, Sussex, England.[10]

      ii.   **Katherine Heasman** was baptized on 6 Feb 1648 in East Grinstead, Sussex, England.[10]

     iii.   **Susannah Heasman** was baptized on 31 Jan 1651 in East Grinstead, Sussex, England.[6]

John next married **Ann Bane** on 2 Dec 1658 in Saint Swithuns, East Grinstead, Sussex, England. [144]

Children from this marriage were:

       i.   **William Heasman** was baptized on 25 Oct 1659 in East Grinstead, Sussex, England.[210]

      ii.   **Elizabeth Heasman** was baptized on 13 Dec 1660 in Saint Swithuns, East Grinstead, Sussex, England.[211]

     iii.   **Elizabeth Heasman** was baptized on 13 Mar 1663 in Saint Swithuns, East Grinstead, Sussex, England[6] and died on 2 Sep 1668 in East Grinstead, Sussex, England[2] at age 5.

     iv.   **Richard Heasman** was baptized on 31 Jul 1665 in Saint Swithuns, East Grinstead, Sussex, England.[144]

  128 v.   **Edward Heasman**

     vi.   **John Heasman** was baptized on 8 Feb 1668 in East Grinstead, Sussex, England[212] and was buried on 10 Feb 1668 in East Grinstead, Sussex, England. [6]

     vii.   **Robert Heasman** was baptized on 30 Apr 1670 in Saint Swithuns, East Grinstead, Sussex, England[212] and was buried on 12 Feb 1746 in East Grinstead, Sussex, England.[2]

    viii.   **Elizabeth Heasman** was baptized on 2 Jan 1673 in East Grinstead, Sussex, England.[6]

257. Ann Bane, daughter of **Cornelius Bane**[10] and **An Cormucke,**[149] was baptized on 21 Feb 1634 in Saint Swithuns, East Grinstead, Sussex, England.[6] Another name for Ann was Ann Bayne.

Ann married **John Heasman** on 2 Dec 1658 in Saint Swithuns, East Grinstead, Sussex, England. [144]

260. William Medhurst, son of **John Medhurst** and **Repentance West,** was baptized on 12 Aug 1636 in All Saints Church, Maidstone, Kent, England[6] and was buried about 1680-1700.[150]

William married **Sarah.**[150]

Children from this marriage were:

       i.   **Sarah Medhurst** was baptized on 19 Oct 1662 in Maidstone, Kent, England[6] and died circa 1703 in Hever, Kent, England[150] about age 41.

      ii.   **Margaret Medhurst**[150] was born about 1663.

       iii.   **Ann Medhurst**[150] was baptized on 16 Apr 1665 in Hartfield, Sussex, England. [10]

130 iv.   **William Medhurst**[150]

       v.   **Mary Medhurst**[150] was baptized on 4 Jan 1669 in Hartfield, Sussex, England. [10]

       vi.   **Thomas Medhurst**[150] was baptized on 4 Apr 1670 in Hartfield, Sussex, England.[10]

       vii.   **Susannah "Susan" Medhurst**[150] was baptized on 17 Apr 1672 in Hartfield, Sussex, England[10] and was buried on 6 May 1710 in East Grinstead, Sussex, England.[125]

       viii.   **Rachell Medhurst** was baptized on 13 Mar 1674 in Hartfield, Sussex, England.

       ix.   **Elizabeth Medhurst** was born circa 1676.

       x.   **Jane Medhurst**[150] was born about 1677 and was buried on 29 Apr 1754 in East Grinstead, Sussex, England.[125]

       xi.   **Edward Medhurst**[150] was baptized on 28 Feb 1678 in Hartfield, Sussex, England.[10]

261. **Sarah**[150] was born about 1642 and was buried on 13 Jan 1720 in Saint Swithuns, East Grinstead, Sussex, England.[2]

Sarah married **William Medhurst.**

262. **George Cornwell Jr.,**[151] son of **George Cornwell** and **Dorothy,**[6] was born about 1643 and was buried on 19 Nov 1703 in Saint Thomas à Becket Church, Framfield, Sussex, England. [5]

    Research Notes: The baptism of his daughter, Mary, says he is a "junior."

George married **Mary** about 1664.

Children from this marriage were:

131 i.   **Elizabeth Cornwell**

       ii.   **Mary Cornwell** was baptized on 19 Jul 1668 in Rotherfield, Sussex, England.[6]

       iii.   **Sarah Cornwell** was baptized on 12 Feb 1670 in Rotherfield, Sussex, England. [10]

       iv.   **George Cornwell** was baptized on 27 May 1673 in Buxted, Sussex, England[10] and was buried on 28 Jun 1733 in Framfield, Sussex, England.[2]

       v.   **William Cornwell** was baptized on 18 Feb 1676 in Buxted, Sussex, England[6] and was buried on 6 Apr 1727 in Framfield, Sussex, England.[2]

       vi.   **John Cornwell** was baptized on 7 Dec 1679 in Buxted, Sussex, England and was buried on 2 Feb 1708 in Framfield, Sussex, England. [125]

263. **Mary** was buried on 17 Feb 1700 in Saint Thomas à Becket Church, Framfield, Sussex, England.[152]

Mary married **George Cornwell Jr.**[151] about 1664.

264. **William Wheatley,** son of **John Wheatley**[155] and **Joan Chatfield,** was baptized on 24 May 1629 in Saint Mary the Virgin Church, Ringmer, Sussex, England[156] and was buried on 12 May 1676 in Saint Marys Church, Barcombe, Sussex, England. [155]

William married **Ann Kidder**[155] on 28 Nov 1654 in Saint Bartholomews Church, Maresfield, Sussex, England.[155]

Children from this marriage were:

132 i.   **Edward Wheatley**[155]

       ii.   **William Wheatley** was baptized on 11 Sep 1659 in Saint Marys Church,

Barcombe, Sussex, England[156] and was buried on 4 Mar 1729 in Uckfield, Sussex, England.[155]

    iii.   **Anne Wheatley** was baptized on 12 Jan 1662 in Saint Marys Church, Barcombe, Sussex, England.[156]

    iv.   **Joane Wheatley** was baptized on 1 May 1664 in Saint Marys Church, Barcombe, Sussex, England.[156]

    v.   **John Wheatley**[155] was baptized on 15 Nov 1668 in Saint Marys Church, Barcombe, Sussex, England.[155]

    vi.   **Drew Wheatley**[155] was baptized on 21 Mar 1675 in Saint Marys Church, Barcombe, Sussex, England.[155]

265. Ann Kidder,[155] daughter of **Drew Kidder** and **Anne Nicholas,** was born circa 1634 in Maresfield, Sussex, England.

    Noted events in her life were:
    • Land: 4 acres called Newlond on Duddleswell Manor, 1684, Maresfield, Sussex, England. [155]

Ann married **William Wheatley** on 28 Nov 1654 in Saint Bartholomews Church, Maresfield, Sussex, England.[155]

272. John Turk was born about 1655 and was buried on 22 Sep 1705 in Saint Denys, Rotherfield, Sussex, England.[125]

    Noted events in his life were:
    • Sale: 1702, Rotherfield, Sussex, England.[213]

John married **Mary** circa 1680.

The child from this marriage was:

    136 i.   **John Turk**

273. Mary was born about 1655 and was buried on 16 Sep 1704 in Saint Denys, Rotherfield, Sussex, England.[125]

Mary married **John Turk** circa 1680.

274. William Browne,[159] son of **William Browne** and **Elizabeth Groombridge,** was born about 1643.

William married **Katherine Longly** on 11 May 1671 in Saint Michaels Church, Withyham, Sussex, England.[12]

Children from this marriage were:

    i.   **John Browne** was baptized on 19 May 1672 in Withyham, Sussex, England[10] and was buried on 17 Jan 1709 in Horsted Keynes, Sussex, England.[2]

    ii.   **Mary Browne** was baptized on 10 Jan 1673 in Withyham, Sussex, England[10] and was buried on 15 Jul 1674 in Withyham, Sussex, England.[160]

    137 iii.   **Sarah Browne**

    iv.   **Katherine Browne** was baptized on 22 Apr 1680 in Withyham, Sussex, England.[1]

    138 v.   **William Browne**

    vi.   **Elizabeth Browne** was baptized on 7 Jun 1684 in Withyham, Sussex, England.[10]

    vii.   **Mary Browne** was baptized on 8 May 1686 in Withyham, Sussex, England.

viii. **Anna Browne** was baptized on 3 Apr 1688 in Withyham, Sussex, England [10] and was buried on 30 Mar 1689 in Withyham, Sussex, England. [160]

ix. **Jane Browne** was baptized on 23 Mar 1689 in Withyham, Sussex, England. [1]

x. **Thomas Browne** was baptized on 5 Jan 1692 in Withyham, Sussex, England [1] and was buried on 12 Oct 1734 in Rotherfield, Sussex, England. [214]

275. Katherine Longly was born about 1650 and was buried on 1 Jun 1722 in Saint Michaels Church, Withyham, Sussex, England. [22]

Katherine married **William Browne** [159] on 11 May 1671 in Saint Michaels Church, Withyham, Sussex, England. [12]

276. William Browne
(Duplicate. See Person 274 on Page 103)

277. Katherine Longly
(Duplicate. See Person 275 on Page 104)

278. John Bridger, son of **John Bridger,** was born circa 1665.

John married **Sarah Coe** on 13 May 1690 in Saint Peter and Saint Paul, Wadhurst, Sussex, England. [16]

Children from this marriage were:

  i. **John Bridger**

139 ii. **Sarah Bridger**

279. Sarah Coe.

Sarah married **John Bridger** on 13 May 1690 in Saint Peter and Saint Paul, Wadhurst, Sussex, England. [16]

290. Robart Pope was born about 1645 and was buried on 24 Jan 1705 in Hartfield, Sussex, England. [2]

Robart married **Ann Plano** on 16 Sep 1669 in Saint Mary the Virgin Church, Hartfield, Sussex, England. [16]

Children from this marriage were:

  i. **Debora Pope** was baptized on 6 Nov 1670 in Hartfield, Sussex, England [6] and was buried in May 1692 in Hartfield, Sussex, England. [125]

145 ii. **Mary Pope**

  iii. **Nicholas Pope** was baptized on 24 Feb 1675 in Hartfield, Sussex, England [6] and was buried on 26 May 1749 in Hartfield, Sussex, England. [215]

  iv. **Edward Pope** was baptized on 14 Dec 1677 in Hartfield, Sussex, England. [6]

  v. **Jane Pope** was baptized on 28 Jan 1681 in Hartfield, Sussex, England [6] and was buried on 15 Sep 1681 in Hartfield, Sussex, England. [125]

  vi. **Ann Pope** was baptized on 23 Sep 1683 in Hartfield, Sussex, England. [6]

  vii. **Jane Pope** was baptized on 23 Sep 1683 in Hartfield, Sussex, England [6] and was buried on 5 Dec 1745 in Hartfield, Sussex, England. [125]

Ancestor Report for Frederick Keith Heasman

291. Ann Plano was born about 1650.

> Research Notes: The Planos were possibly French Protestants.

Ann married **Robart Pope** on 16 Sep 1669 in Saint Mary the Virgin Church, Hartfield, Sussex, England.[16]

296. Thomas Wood, son of **John Wood**[10] and **Joane,**[10] was baptized on 18 Oct 1632 in East Grinstead, Sussex, England.[10]

Thomas married **Elizabeth Croft** on 19 Nov 1663 in East Grinstead, Sussex, England.[12]

Children from this marriage were:

	i.	**Mary Wood** was baptized on 24 May 1665 in East Grinstead, Sussex, England.[10]
	ii.	**Elizabeth Wood** was baptized on 27 Aug 1667 in East Grinstead, Sussex, England.[10]
	iii.	**Thomas Wood** was baptized on 15 Feb 1669 in East Grinstead, Sussex, England.[10]
148	iv.	**Thomas Wood**
	v.	**Elizabeth Wood** was baptized on 24 Jan 1672 in East Grinstead, Sussex, England.[10]
	vi.	**Robert Wood** was baptized on 24 Jan 1672 in East Grinstead, Sussex, England.[10]
	vii.	**Sarah Wood** was baptized on 9 Oct 1675 in East Grinstead, Sussex, England.[10]

297. Elizabeth Croft, daughter of **Richard Crofte**[6] and **Ann,**[6] was baptized on 27 Jun 1643 in East Grinstead, Sussex, England.[10]

Elizabeth married **Thomas Wood** on 19 Nov 1663 in East Grinstead, Sussex, England.[12]

298. Arthur Marchant was buried on 15 Feb 1676 in Rotherfield, Sussex, England.[125]

Arthur married **Mary Winder** on 21 Nov 1672 in Buxted, Sussex, England.[5]

Children from this marriage were:

	i.	**Arthur Marchant** was baptized on 30 Nov 1673 in Rotherfield, Sussex, England.[10]
149	ii.	**Mary Marchant**[10]

299. Mary Winder was buried on 12 Aug 1721 in Rotherfield, Sussex, England.[125]

Mary married **Arthur Marchant** on 21 Nov 1672 in Buxted, Sussex, England.[5]

Mary next married **Christopher Parkes** on 23 Nov 1676 in Rotherfield, Sussex, England.[12]

330. William Smith[137] was born about 1670.

> Noted events in his life were:
> • Resided: 1696, Steep, Hampshire, England.[137]

William married someone.

His children were:

165	i.	**Frances Smith**
	ii.	**William Smith** was baptized on 10 Apr 1696 in Steep, Hampshire, England.[137]

Ancestor Report for Frederick Keith Heasman

Tenth Generation (7th Great-Grandparents)

512. Francis Heasman, son of **William Heasman** and **Elizabeth Cayley,** was born circa 1590 in Sussex, England and was buried on 2 Jan 1667 in Saint Margarets Church, West Hoathly, Sussex, England.[145]

Birth Notes: Probably born in Barcombe or Little Horsted in Sussex.

General Notes:
Francis Heasman was keeper of Hindleap, which was the northwestern part of Ashdown forest near East Grinstead. Francis maintained Hindleap for royal hunts.

Research Notes:
Ashdown Forest was an ancient, royal hunting park of about 20 squares situated 30 miles south of London. In the 1200s the forest was enclosed by a pale (a fence with an interior ditch) to keep the deer inside. By the late 1300s Ashdown was also called Lancaster Great Park.
In the early 1600s, the forest was managed by keepers whose duties were similar to a modern park ranger and game warden. The keepers' lived on sections of the forest called Southward, Pippingford, Hindleap, Broadstone, Coombedean, and Whitedean. The keepers -- usually gentlemen -- were given lodges, a few dozen acres, and out buildings.[216]

Noted events in his life were:
- Resided: a gentleman, before 1610, Horsted Parva, Sussex, England.[217]
- Occupation: keeper of Hindleap Walk, 1610-1657, Hindleap Lodge, Forest Row, East Grinstead, Sussex, England.[218]
- Land: inherited land from his father, 1616-1617, Barcombe, Sussex, England.[219]
- Letters Patent: reappointed keeper, 16 May 1646, Hindleap Lodge, Forest Row, East Grinstead, Sussex, England.[220]
- Survey: Parliamentary Survey No. 26, 1650, Hindleap Lodge, Forest Row, East Grinstead, Sussex, England.[221]
- Survey: Survey of Sussex No. 12, 1657, Hindleap Lodge, Forest Row, East Grinstead, Sussex, England.[222]

Francis married **Bridget Foord** on 4 Jun 1610 in All Saints Church, Lewes, Sussex, England.[146]

Children from this marriage were:

	i.	**Frances Heasman** was baptized on 21 Jul 1611 in Buxted, Sussex, England.[223]
	ii.	**Thomas Heasman** was baptized on 10 Apr 1617 in Saint Margaret the Queen Church, Buxted, Sussex, England.[223]
	iii.	**John Heasman** was baptized on 20 Dec 1619 in Saint Swithuns, East Grinstead, Sussex, England.[6]
256	iv.	**John Heasman**
	v.	**Rose Heasman** was baptized on 29 Jan 1624 in Saint Swithuns, East Grinstead, Sussex, England.[6]
	vi.	**Elsabeth Heasman** was baptized on 27 Mar 1626 in Saint Swithuns, East Grinstead, Sussex, England.[10]
	vii.	**Anthony Heasman** was baptized on 3 Feb 1629 in Saint Swithuns, East Grinstead, Sussex, England.[10]
	viii.	**An Heasman** was baptized on 20 Jun 1631 in Saint Swithuns, East Grinstead, Sussex, England.[10]

Ancestor Report for Frederick Keith Heasman

513. Bridget Foord, daughter of **John Foord,** was born circa 1590 in Sussex, England[147] and was buried on 14 Jan 1669 in Saint Margarets Church, West Hoathly, Sussex, England.[148]

> Birth Notes: Probably born in Buxted, Sussex.

> Noted events in her life were:
> • Resided: wed as maiden, 1610, Buxted, Sussex, England.[217]

Bridget married **Francis Heasman** on 4 Jun 1610 in All Saints Church, Lewes, Sussex, England.[146]

514. Cornelius Bane[10] was born about 1610.

> Noted events in his life were:
> • Occupation: freemason, 1639, East Grinstead, Sussex, England.[161]

Cornelius married **An Cormucke**[149] about 1630.

Children from this marriage were:

	i.	**Elenor Bane** was baptized on 3 Jul 1631 in East Grinstead, Sussex, England.[144]
257	ii.	**Ann Bane**
	iii.	**John Bane** was baptized on 19 Feb 1637 in East Grinstead, Sussex, England.[144]
	iv.	**Richard Bane** was baptized on 27 Jan 1639 in East Grinstead, Sussex, England.[144]
	v.	**Cornelius Bane** was baptized on 26 Mar 1640.[144]
	vi.	**Mary Bane** was baptized on 27 Nov 1642 in East Grinstead, Sussex, England.[224]

515. An Cormucke.[149]

An married **Cornelius Bane**[10] about 1630.

520. John Medhurst was born circa 1615.

John married **Repentance West** on 11 Oct 1635 in All Saints Church, Maidstone, Kent, England.[153]

The child from this marriage was:

> 260 i. **William Medhurst**

521. Repentance West.

Repentance married **John Medhurst** on 11 Oct 1635 in All Saints Church, Maidstone, Kent, England.[153]

Repentance next married **Edward Kemte** on 17 Jan 1642 in Maidstone, Kent, England.[225]

524. George Cornwell died circa 1693 in Framfield, Sussex, England.[154] Another name for George was Jorge.

> Research Notes: There are several Cromwell families in the area with the same first names. They were not farmers, but were craftsmen, carpenters, spoon makers, pail makers, etc. They moved several times to work at different estates.

George married **Dorothy.**[6]

Children from this marriage were:

> i. **John Cornwell**[226] died circa 1715.[227]

    ii.   **Robert Cornwell**[228]
    iii.   **William Cornwell**[228]
262 iv.   **George Cornwell Jr.**[151]

525. Dorothy.[6]

Dorothy married **George Cornwell**.

528. John Wheatley[155] died circa 1654.[155]

> Research Notes: He could be the John Wheatley mentioned in a 1623 survey of Ringmer's Broyle manor commissioned by James I. Wheatley gave testimony regarding the condition and use of the land by farmers. [229]

> Noted events in his life were:
> • Occupation: husbandman, 1620, Ringmer, Sussex, England.[230]
>
> • Status: yeoman, 1626, Ringmer, Sussex, England.[230]

John married **Argent Gower** on 15 May 1620 in Saint Thomas-à-Becket at Cliffe Church, Lewes, Sussex, England.[157]

The child from this marriage was:

    i.   **Mary Wheatley** was baptized on 22 Jul 1621 in All Saints, Laughton, Sussex, England.[6]

John next married **Joan Chatfield** on 24 Aug 1626 in Saint Thomas-à-Becket at Cliffe Church, Lewes, Sussex, England.[157]

Children from this marriage were:

    i.   **John Wheatley** was baptized on 12 Aug 1627 in Saint Mary the Virgin Church, Ringmer, Sussex, England[156] and died in 1685 at age 58.
264 ii.   **William Wheatley**
    iii. **Jone Wheatley** was baptized on 31 Aug 1634 in Saint Mary the Virgin Church, Ringmer, Sussex, England.[156]
    iv. **Thomas Wheatley** was baptized on 20 Dec 1635 in Saint Mary the Virgin Church, Ringmer, Sussex, England.[156]
    v.   **Elizabeth Wheatley** was baptized on 8 Sep 1639 in Saint Mary the Virgin Church, Ringmer, Sussex, England.[156]

529. Joan Chatfield was baptized on 20 Jun 1591 in Saint Peters Church, Chailey, Sussex, England and was buried on 15 Jan 1653 in Saint Mary the Virgin Church, Ringmer, Sussex, England.[157]

> Noted events in her life were:
> • Resided: 1626, Ringmer, Sussex, England.[230]

Joan married **John Wheatley**[155] on 24 Aug 1626 in Saint Thomas-à-Becket at Cliffe Church, Lewes, Sussex, England.[157]

530. Drew Kidder died about 1650 in Maresfield, Sussex, England.[158]

> Research Notes: He was probably a descendent or relative of Richard Kidder of Maresfield, Sussex, England,

Ancestor Report for Frederick Keith Heasman

living in 1492.

Noted events in his life were:
• Will: 1650.[218]

Drew married **Anne Nicholas** on 31 Aug 1629 in Saint Margaret the Queen Church, Buxted, Sussex, England.[155]

Children from this marriage were:

   265   i.   **Ann Kidder**[155]
        ii.   **Drew Kidder**
        iii.   **John Kidder**
        iv.   **Elizabeth Kidder**

531. Anne Nicholas died in 1678 in Maresfield, Sussex, England.[155]

Noted events in her life were:
• Land: barn and 4 acres called Newlond on Duddleswell Manor, 1659, Maresfield, Sussex, England.[155]

Anne married **Drew Kidder** on 31 Aug 1629 in Saint Margaret the Queen Church, Buxted, Sussex, England.[155]

Anne next married **William Attree**[155] before 1665.[155]

548. William Browne was born circa 1620 and was buried on 10 Mar 1674 in Saint Michaels Church, Withyham, Sussex, England.[160]

Noted events in his life were:
• Occupation: husbandman, Withyham, Sussex, England.[161]

• Will: 1674, Withyham, Sussex, England.[231]

William married **Elizabeth Groombridge** on 19 Jul 1640 in Saint John sub Castro Church, Lewes, Sussex, England.[161]

Children from this marriage were:

        i.   **Ralph Browne**[159] was buried on 11 Mar 1732 in Withyham, Sussex, England.[125]
        ii.   **Thomas Browne**[159] was buried on 11 Jul 1710 in Withyham, Sussex, England.[160]
        iii.   **Sarah Browne**[159]
        iv.   **Richard Browne**[159] was baptized on 21 Mar 1640 in Withyham, Sussex, England.[6]
        v.   **Joan Browne**[159]
   274 vi.   **William Browne**[159]

549. Elizabeth Groombridge, daughter of **Ralph Groombridge** and **Joan Richardson**,[172] was born circa 1620 and was buried on 20 Feb 1684 in Saint Michaels Church, Withyham, Sussex, England.[160]

Noted events in her life were:
• Resided: 1640, Rotherfield, Sussex, England.[161]

• Will: 1683, Withyham, Sussex, England.[159]

Ancestor Report for Frederick Keith Heasman

Elizabeth married **William Browne** on 19 Jul 1640 in Saint John sub Castro Church, Lewes, Sussex, England.[161]

556. John Bridger was born about 1640, died in 1722[162] about age 82, and was buried on 3 Oct 1722.[2]

> Noted events in his life were:
> • Will: 9 Feb 1721, Lewes, Sussex, England.[162]

John married someone.

His children were:

	i.	**Elizabeth Bridger** was born about 1665.
278	ii.	**John Bridger**

592. John Wood,[10] son of **John Wood** and **Sicely**,[10] was baptized on 5 Jul 1608 in East Grinstead, Sussex, England[10] and was buried on 1 Jun 1669 in East Grinstead, Sussex, England.[125]

John married **Joane**.[10]

Children from this marriage were:

	i.	**John Wood** was baptized on 2 Dec 1630 in East Grinstead, Sussex, England.[10]
296	ii.	**Thomas Wood**
	iii.	**Richard Wood** was baptized on 31 Aug 1634 in East Grinstead, Sussex, England.[10]
	iv.	**Elizabeth Wood** was baptized on 6 Aug 1637 in East Grinstead, Sussex, England.[10]
	v.	**Jone Wood**[10] was baptized on 12 Jan 1640 in East Grinstead, Sussex, England.

593. Joane.[10]

Joane married **John Wood**.[10]

594. Richard Crofte,[6] son of **Richard Crofte**[10] and **Annis Gatland**,[173] was baptized in Aug 1619 in East Grinstead, Sussex, England.[10]

> Research Notes: His children's birth records say his wife is An, but many researchers say it is Elizabeth Browne. Are An and Elizabeth the same person?

Richard married **Ann**.[6]

Children from this marriage were:

	i.	**Mary Croft** was baptized on 4 Apr 1641 in East Grinstead, Sussex, England.[6]
297	ii.	**Elizabeth Croft**

595. Ann.[6]

Ann married **Richard Crofte**.[6]

11th Generation (8th Great-Grandparents)

1024. William Heasman, son of **John Heasman**[168] and **Alice,**[170] was born circa Jan 1551[165] and died in 1616 in Little Horsted, Sussex, England[166] about age 65. Another name for William was William Heseman.

Death Notes: His son Francis inherited the freehold at Rodmell, but he did no inherit any animals.

General Notes:
William Heseman was a freeholder on the estate of Rodmell in Barcombe. As a freeholder, he owned his land outright. William was a gentleman, an untitled member of the English gentry. His 60 acres in Barcombe, which included a barn, was on land called Lakers and Newlands. William owned farm land there from about 1580 to his death in 1616. Today the land is located on Hewen Street NW in Sewells Farm.

Research Notes: There is a record of William Heasman marrying Elizabeth Cayley in 1585, but his will says Ann is his wife. Most likely he married twice, and Elizabeth was the mother of his children.

Noted events in his life were:
- Land: inherited his father's land when he reached legal age, 1572, Barcombe, Sussex, England.[165]

- Tenement: on manor of Rodmell, 1583, Barcombe, Sussex, England.[219]

- Land: took the oath of fidelity to the lord of the manor (fealty) for a freehold tenement, 1587, Barcombe, Sussex, England.[219]

- Legal action: defaulter at Rodmell court, 1593-1614, Barcombe, Sussex, England.[219]

- Land: tenant surrenders land at manor of Rodmell, 1610, Barcombe, Sussex, England.[219]

- Fact: called a gent (gentleman), 1614, Barcombe, Sussex, England.[219]

- Land: surrender of tenement at the manor of Rodmell, 1615, Barcombe, Sussex, England.[219]

- Will: 1615, Little Horsted, Sussex, England.[232]

William married **Elizabeth Cayley** on 8 Jun 1585 in Saint Margaret the Queen Church, Buxted, Sussex, England.[167]

Children from this marriage were:

	i.	**Anne Heasman**[232] was born circa 1589.
512	ii.	**Francis Heasman**
	iii.	**Susan Heasman**[232] was born circa 1591.
	iv.	**Mary Heasman**[232] was born circa 1595.

William next married **Anne**[232] after 1585.

Noted events in her life were:
- Will: 1615, Little Horsted, Sussex, England.[232]

1025. Elizabeth Cayley was born about 1565.

Elizabeth married **William Heasman** on 8 Jun 1585 in Saint Margaret the Queen Church, Buxted, Sussex, England.[167]

1026. John Foord was born about 1560.

Noted events in his life were:
• Resided: as yeoman, 1610, Buxted, Sussex, England. [233]

John married someone.

His child was:

    513   i.   **Bridget Foord**

1098. Ralph Groombridge was born circa 1595 and died in 1646 in Withyham, Sussex, England[171] about age 51. Another name for Ralph was Ralfe Groombredge.

Noted events in his life were:
• Resided: yeoman, 1636, Withyham, Sussex, England. [161]

Ralph married **Joan Richardson**[172] on 11 Dec 1615 in Saint Denys, Rotherfield, Sussex, England.[16]

Children from this marriage were:

       i.   **Ralph Groombridge** was born about 1616.
    549 ii.   **Elizabeth Groombridge**
     iii.   **Margaret Groombridge**[172]

1099. Joan Richardson[172] was born circa 1595.

Joan married **Ralph Groombridge** on 11 Dec 1615 in Saint Denys, Rotherfield, Sussex, England. [16]

1184. John Wood was baptized on 21 May 1586 in East Grinstead, Sussex, England[10] and was buried on 12 Jun 1625 in East Grinstead, Sussex, England.[2] Another name for John was John Woodde.

John married **Sicely**.[10]

Children from this marriage were:

    592 i.   **John Wood**[10]
      ii.   **Richard Wood**[10] was baptized on 24 Feb 1613 in East Grinstead, Sussex, England.
     iii.   **Sicely Wood** was baptized on 30 Nov 1615 in East Grinstead, Sussex, England.[10]
     iv.   **Mary Wood** was baptized on 11 Oct 1618 in East Grinstead, Sussex, England. [10]
      v.   **Elianor Wood** was baptized on 19 Aug 1621 in East Grinstead, Sussex, England.[10]

1185. Sicely[10] was born circa 1588.

Sicely married **John Wood**.

1188. Richard Crofte[10] was baptized on 9 Jun 1594 in East Grinstead, Sussex, England. [6]

Richard married **Annis Gatland**[173] on 24 Feb 1617 in East Grinstead, Sussex, England. [12]

Children from this marriage were:

       i.   **Tobias Crofte**[10] was baptized on 14 Aug 1617 in East Grinstead, Sussex, England.[10]

     ii.   **Ann Crofte** was baptized on 24 Jan 1619 in East Grinstead, Sussex, England. [10]

594 iii.   **Richard Crofte**[6]

     iv.   **Mary Crofte** was baptized on 27 Jan 1622 in East Grinstead, Sussex, England. [10]

1189. Annis Gatland,[173] daughter of **William Gatland,** was baptized on 19 Dec 1591 in Rotherfield, Sussex, England. [10] Another name for Annis was Ann Gatland.

Annis married **Richard Crofte**[10] on 24 Feb 1617 in East Grinstead, Sussex, England. [12]

Ancestor Report for Frederick Keith Heasman

12th Generation (9th Great-Grandparents)

2048. John Heasman[168] died in May 1558 in Barcombe, Sussex, England.[169]

Noted events in his life were:
• Land: 1558, Barcombe, Sussex, England.[165]

• Occupation: husbandman, 1558, Barcombe, Sussex, England.[170]

John married **Alice**.[170]

Children from this marriage were:

        i.   **Jone Heasman**[168] was born about 1545 and died in 1568 in Little Horsted, Sussex, England[234] about age 23.

        ii.   **John Heasman**[234] was born about 1548.

1024 iii.   **William Heasman**

2049. Alice.[170] Another name for Alice is Alys.

Alice married **John Heasman**.[168]

2378. William Gatland.[10]

William married someone.

His children were:

        i.   **Elizabeth Gatland** was baptized on 9 Oct 1586 in East Grinstead, Sussex, England.[10]

        ii.   **William Gatland** was baptized on 12 Nov 1587 in East Grinstead, Sussex, England.[10]

        iii.   **James Gatland**[10] was baptized in 1590 in Rotherfield, Sussex, England.[10]

1189 iv.   **Annis Gatland**[173]

        v.   **Alice Gatland** was baptized on 27 Dec 1593 in Rotherfield, Sussex, England.[10]

        vi.   **Roberte Gatland** was baptized in 1596 in Rotherfield, Sussex, England.[10]

        vii.   **Mary Gatland**[10] was baptized in 1596 in Rotherfield, Sussex, England.

        viii.   **Martha Gatland** was baptized on 10 Sep 1598 in Rotherfield, Sussex, England.[10]

Gallery: Fermanagh County, Ireland

Kerrs circa 1650 to 1862

Lower Lough Erne at Carrickreagh

This is a postcard showing farmland on the shore of the Lower Lough Erne. The lake is part of the River Erne which flows into the Atlantic. The Kerrs had a farm in Carrick, Fermanagh, about a mile inland and a mile north of Derrygonnelly. Carrickreagh in this postcard is just east of Derrygonnelly.

Gallery: Fermanagh County, Ireland

Kerrs circa 1650 to 1862

Ruins of Tully Castle at Tully Point

Tully Castle lies east of Carrick, Fermanagh, on Tully Point. The castle was built for
Sir John Hume who occupied the house until 1641 when it was attacked and burned
on Christmas Eve by Rory Maguire and the inhabitants massacred. It was not lived in
again. Credit: Kenneth Allen.
(2006)

Gallery: Fermanagh County, Ireland

Kerrs circa 1650 to 1862

Main Street in Derrygonnelly

Derrygonnelly is a small market town near the Lower Lough Erne. The main street
was built in 1812 along the Sillees River. Immigrant Andrew Kerr lived on Main
Street where he leased a home with a garden.
(1968)

SS Jura wrecked near Liverpool

Andrew Kerr, his wife, Jane, and their daughter, Jennie, traveled on the SS Jura in March 1862 from Londonderry, Ireland, to Canada. The trip took eleven days. The illustration above shows the ship two years later when it ran ashore. Credit: The Illustrated London News
(1864)

Gallery: Sussex County, England

Heasmans circa 1500 to circa 1860

Middle Row in East Grinstead

This is a view of a row of 14th-century timber-framed buildings called Middle Row located on High Street. Credit: H. T. Melville and East Grinstead Museum (1883)

Gallery: Sussex County, England

Heasmans circa 1500 to circa 1860

Toll Gate in East Grinstead

This photograph is a view of the East Grinstead Toll Gate. The toll-gate, which was situated at the southern end of the town, was removed some time after 1865 when the London-East Grinstead Turnpike Trust was fully funded. The Toll House is the low building on the left. The tower of Saint Swithun's church can be seen center-right.
Credit: William Harding
(1864)

Gallery: Sussex County, England

Heasmans circa 1500 to circa 1860

Lewes Road in East Grinstead

This postcard is a view of Lewes Road, East Grinstead, with St Swithun's Church in the background. Credit: William Page
(1905)

Heasmans circa 1500 to circa 1860

St. Swithun's Church in East Grinstead

St. Swithun's Church, shown in this drawing, was built in the 1300s and 1400s. It was struck by lightning in 1772, and it's tower collapsed in 1785. After replacing the tower and rebuilding some walls, it was re-opened in 1789.
(1781)

Gallery: Sussex County, England

Heasmans circa 1500 to circa 1860

Hindleap Lodge

Hindleap Lodge was occupied by Francis Heasman and his family in the 1600s when he was forest keeper. Credit: Kate Crosby
(2011)

Gallery: Sussex County, England

Heasmans circa 1500 to circa 1860

Village Sign in Coleman's Hatch

Rebecca Swanson stands next to the the village sign for Coleman's Hatch at
Shepherd's Hill Road and Coach Road.
(2008)

Gallery: Sussex County, England

Heasmans circa 1500 to circa 1860

Hatch Inn in Coleman's Hatch

The Hatch Inn (previously Colemans Hatch Public House) was established in the
1700s in a 1430s low-beamed cottage row. It has been an inn for over 200 years.
Credit: Rebecca Swanson
(2008)

Heasmans circa 1500 to circa 1860

St. Mary's Church in Hartfield

The oldest part of the current church building, the nave, was built in the 1200s. The tower was built in the 1300s, but its shingled spire was built in the 1400s. Credit: Rebecca Swanson
(2008)

Gallery: Sussex County, England

Heasmans circa 1500 to circa 1860

High Street in Hartfield

Hartfield is a small village on the northeast edge of Ashdown Forest and the former
home of A.A. Milne. Credit: Rebecca Swanson
(2008)

Bolebroke Castle in Hartfield

Bolebroke Castle, built in the 1400s, was a royal hunting lodge in Hartfield. Henry VIII used the lodge during hunts in Ashdown Forest. It is a private residence today. (1782)

Gallery: Sussex County, England

Heasmans circa 1500 to circa 1860

Hever Castle In Hever, Kent

Hever Castle is located in Hever village six miles north of Hartfield. Built in the
1200s, Hever Castle was the childhood home of Anne Boleyn, second wife of Henry
VIII and mother of Elizabeth I. Credit: Christoph Matthias Siebenborn
(2014)

Gallery: Hampshire County, England

Heasmans circa 1860 to 1873

Ropley Station in Ropley

Ropley Railway Station was opened in 1865 by the Mid-Hants (Alton Lines) Railway. The station was closed to regular service by British Rail in 1973 and reopened as part of the historic Watercress Line in 1977.
(1975)

Gallery: Hampshire County, England

Heasmans circa 1860 to 1873

Little Barton Farm cottage in Ropley

The Little Barton thatched cottage in Ropley is an example of housing for
agricultural laborers in the 1700s and 1800s. Little Barton had three bedrooms,
earthen floors, and a central fireplace. Three families -- 15 or 20 people -- would have
crowded into those three rooms. The cottage is now a private residence.
(circa 1880)

Heasmans circa 1860 to 1873

Fulling Mill in Alresford

The Fulling Mill across the River Alre in Alresford was built in the 1200s. "Fulling" is the cleansing of cloth (particularly wool) to eliminate oils, dirt, and other impurities, and making it thicker. Water power was used to drive hammers to clean the cloth. Credit: Tristram Biggs
(2015)

Gallery: Cobourg, Northumberland County, Ontario, Canada

Kerrs 1862-1894 and Heasmans 1873-1894

King Street in Cobourg, Ontario

Postcard of King Street in downtown Cobourg. Nellie Kerr and F.H. Heasman lived
in Cobourg before they were married in America.
(1930)

Gallery: Cobourg, Northumberland County, Ontario, Canada

Kerrs 1862-1894 and Heasmans 1873-1894

Ontario Woollen Mills in Cobourg, Ontario

F.H. Heasman and some of his siblings worked at the Ontario Woollen Mills in
Cobourg. The Woollen Mills was the largest industry in Cobourg for most of the
1800s. At its peak it manufactured over 400,000 yards of cloth a year and was one of
the largest industries of its kind in Canada.
(circa 1905)

Gallery: Cobourg, Northumberland County, Ontario, Canada

Kerrs 1862-1894 and Heasmans 1873-1894

Victoria Hall in Cobourg, Ontario

The ornate Victoria Hall in Cobourg was built between 1856 and 1860. It contained the town's administrative and government offices, as well as a council chamber, a court room, judge's chambers, offices, a concert hall for 1000 people, community meeting rooms, law offices and Masonic lodge rooms.
(1860)

Gallery: Conneaut, Ashtabula County, Ohio

Kerrs and Heasmans after 1899

Main Street in Conneaut, Ohio

Postcard of Main Street in Conneaut, Ohio, taken about the time the Heasmans
moved to town.
(circa 1900)

Kerrs and Heasmans after 1899

Hulett Ore Unloader in Conneaut, Ohio

The Hulett Automatic Ore Unloader was invented by George H. Hulett, a native of
Conneaut, in the late 1800's. It allowed rapid unloading of cargo and increased the
volume and efficiency of the ore docks. In 1899, the first working Hulett machine
installed at Conneaut Harbor in Conneaut, Ohio.
(about 1900)

Gallery: Conneaut, Ashtabula County, Ohio

Kerrs and Heasmans after 1899

Baldwin/Heasman block building in Conneaut, Ohio

This building was constructed on the corner of Main and Mill Streets by the Baldwins
and purchased by F.H. Heasman in 1911. The first floor had stores, the second floor
had apartments, and the third floor had a performance hall used for plays and dances.
Credit: Conneaut Library and Jeff Lebzelter
(circa 1900)

Announcement of Heasman store relocation

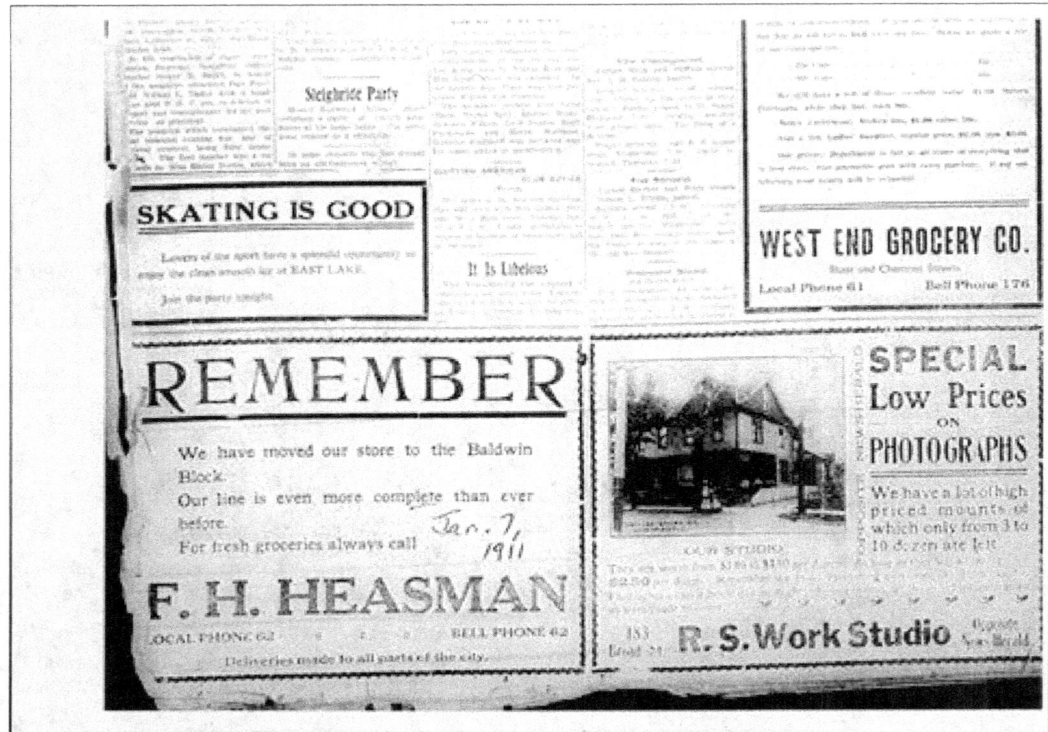

This advertisement announces the relocation of Heasman's Grocery to the Baldwin Block in January 1911. Credit: Conneaut Library and Jeff Lebzelter
(1911)

Gallery: Conneaut, Ashtabula County, Ohio

Kerrs and Heasmans after 1899

Heasman's Grocery delivery cart

Heasman's Grocery home delivery cart in front of the store. Credit: Cindy Burns
Eigel's collection.
(circa 1920)

Gallery: Conneaut, Ashtabula County, Ohio

Kerrs and Heasmans after 1899

Heasman's store advertisement

Credit: Conneaut Library and Jeff Lebzelter
(1920)

People in front of the Heasman's Grocery in Conneaut, Ohio

Credit: Cindy Burns Eigel's collection.

Gallery: Conneaut, Ashtabula County, Ohio

Kerrs and Heasmans after 1899

Heasman Block buildings about to meet the wrecking ball

Credit: Doug Murphy
(Oct 1964)

Gallery: Conneaut, Ashtabula County, Ohio

Kerrs and Heasmans after 1899

Heasman Block (left building) and Main Street homes

Heasman Block and homes before they was demolished for a chain grocery store.
Credit: Doug Murphy
(Oct 1964)

Gallery: Conneaut, Ashtabula County, Ohio

Kerrs and Heasmans after 1899

Newspaper picture of razing of Heasman Block

Credit: Conneaut Library and Jeff Lebzelter
(1964)

Gallery: Conneaut, Ashtabula County, Ohio

Kerrs and Heasmans after 1899

Heasman family monument at Glenwood Cemetery in Conneat, Ohio

Gallery: Conneaut, Ashtabula County, Ohio

Kerrs and Heasmans after 1899

Gravestone of Keith Heasman in Glenwood Cemetery, Conneaut

Gallery: Conneaut, Ashtabula County, Ohio

Kerrs and Heasmans after 1899

Nellie (Kerr) Heasman's gravestone in Glenwood Cemetery, Conneaut

Gallery: Kerr Family Pictures

The Kerr sisters in Cobourg, Ontario

On the right is Margaret Jane "Jennie" (1861-1937); on the top is Mary Ann (abt 1863-); on the left is Elinor "Nellie" (1870-1918), and on the bottom is Charlotte Elizabeth "Lottie" (abt 1880-).
(about 1890)

Gallery: Kerr Family Pictures

F.H. Heasman and Nellie Kerr

F.H. Heasman and Nellie Kerr about the time of their wedding. Credit: Rebecca
Swanson's collection.
(circa 1895)

Gallery: Kerr Family Pictures

F.H. and Nellie Heasman's family

On the left is Nellie (Kerr) Heasman; on the right is F.H. Heasman; on the top is
Keith Heasman; and on the bottom is Darrell Heasman. Credit: Cindy Burns Eigel's
collection.
(about 1915)

Gallery: Heasman Family Pictures

Four Generations of Heasmans

Left is F.H. Heasman; seated is his mother Emma (Stubbs) Heasman; right is Keith
Heasman; the baby is Keith's daughter, eight-month-old Patricia Heasman. This
photograph was taken in Toronto, Canada. Credit: Rebecca Swanson's collection.
(Jun 1925)

Gallery: Heasman Family Pictures

F.H. Heasman

F.H. Heasman (Keith and Red Heasman's father) was the founder of Heasman's
Grocery in Conneaut, Ohio. Credit: Cindy Burns Eigel's collection.
(about 1915)

Gallery: Heasman Family Pictures

William Heasman and his wife

F.H. Heasman's brother, William, lived with F.H. in Conneaut. Later, William opened a women's fashion store in Moosejaw, Canada. Credit: Rebecca Swanson's collection.
(circa 1940)

Gallery: Heasman Family Pictures

F.H. Heasman

F.H. Heasman with his grandaughters Patricia Ann, daughter of Keith Heasman, and
Mary Ann, daughter of Red Heasman. Credit: Rebecca Swanson's collection.
(about 1935)

Gallery: Heasman Family Pictures

F.H. and Gertrude Heasman

F.H. Heasman and his second wife, Gertrude Zundel. Credit: Rebecca Swanson's
collection.
(circa 1950)

Gallery: Heasman Family Pictures

F.H. Heasman

F.H. Heasman with his dog Josephine. Credit: Rebecca Swanson's collection.
(circa 1950)

Gallery: Heasman Family Pictures

Fannie (Heasman) and David Reid

Fannie (Heasman) Reid, sister of F.H. Heasman, with her husband, David Reid.
Credit: Rebecca Swanson's collection.

Gallery: Heasman Family Pictures

Fannie (Heasman) Reid and Partricia Ann Heasman

Fannie (Heasman) Reid, sister of F.H. Heasman, with her niece, Partricia Ann
Heasman. Credit: Rebecca Swanson's collection.
(1936)

Gallery: Heasman Family Pictures

Keith Heasman and Marion Rodgers

Keith Heasman and Marion Rodgers in a Ford Model T two years before they were married. Credit: Rebecca Swanson's collection.
(1917)

Gallery: Heasman Family Pictures

Darrell "Red" Heasman

Darrell "Red" Heasman in the meat department at Heasman's Grocery. Credit: Cindy Burns Eigel's collection.

Gallery: Heasman Family Pictures

Laura and Mary Ann Heasman

Laura (Hogle) Heasman (wife of Darrell "Red" Heasman) with her daughter, Mary Ann, in front of Heasman's Grocery. Credit: Cindy Burns Eigel's collection.
(about 1935)

Gallery: Heasman Family Pictures

Mary Ann Heasman

Mary Ann Heasman, daughter of Darrell "Red" and Laura Heasman, in front of the
Heasman's Grocery. Credit: Cindy Burns Eigel's collection.
(about 1933)

Gallery: Heasman Family Pictures

Gertrude (Zundel) Heasman

F.H. Heasman's second wife, Gertrude (Zundel) Heasman, with Jimmy and Cindy Burns. Her apartment was in the Heasman building above the stores. Credit: Cindy Burns Eigel's collection.

Gallery: Heasman Family Pictures

Keith and Patricia Heasman

Keith Heasman and his daughter, Patricia. Credit: Rebecca Swanson's collection.
(1936)

Gallery: Heasman Family Pictures

Patricia and Keith Heasman

Keith Heasman and his daughter, Patricia, on vacation in Canada. Credit: Rebecca Swanson's collection.
(1940)

Gallery: Heasman Family Pictures

Patricia and Keith Heasman

Keith Heasman and his daughter, Patricia, on vacation in Canada. Credit: Rebecca Swanson's collection.
(1940)

Gallery: Heasman Family Pictures

Keith and Patricia Heasman

Keith and his daughter, Patricia, on vacation at the beach in Cobourg, Ontario.
Credit: Rebecca Swanson's collection.
(1940)

Gallery: Heasman Family Pictures

Keith and Marion Heasman

Keith and Marion Heasman on vacation at the beach in Cobourg, Ontario. Credit:
Rebecca Swanson's collection.
(1940)

Gallery: Heasman Family Pictures

Keith and Marion Heasman

Keith and Marion Heasman on vacation in Canada. Credit: Rebecca Swanson's collection.
(1940)

Gallery: Heasman Family Pictures

Patricia and Keith Heasman

Keith Heasman and his daughter, Patricia, on vacation in Cobourg, Ontario. Credit:
Rebecca Swanson's collection.
(1940)

Gallery: Heasman Family Pictures

Keith and Marion Heasman

Keith and Marion Heasman in Conneaut. Credit: Rebecca Swanson's collection.
(1936)

Gallery: Heasman Family Pictures

Keith and Marion Heasman

Keith and Marion Heasman in Conneaut. Credit: Rebecca Swanson's collection.
(circa 1950)

Gallery: Heasman Family Pictures

Keith Heasman and Rebecca Eagles

Keith Heasman holds his grandaughter, Rebecca Eagles. Credit: Rebecca Swanson's collection.
(1952)

Gallery: Heasman Family Pictures

Keith Heasman

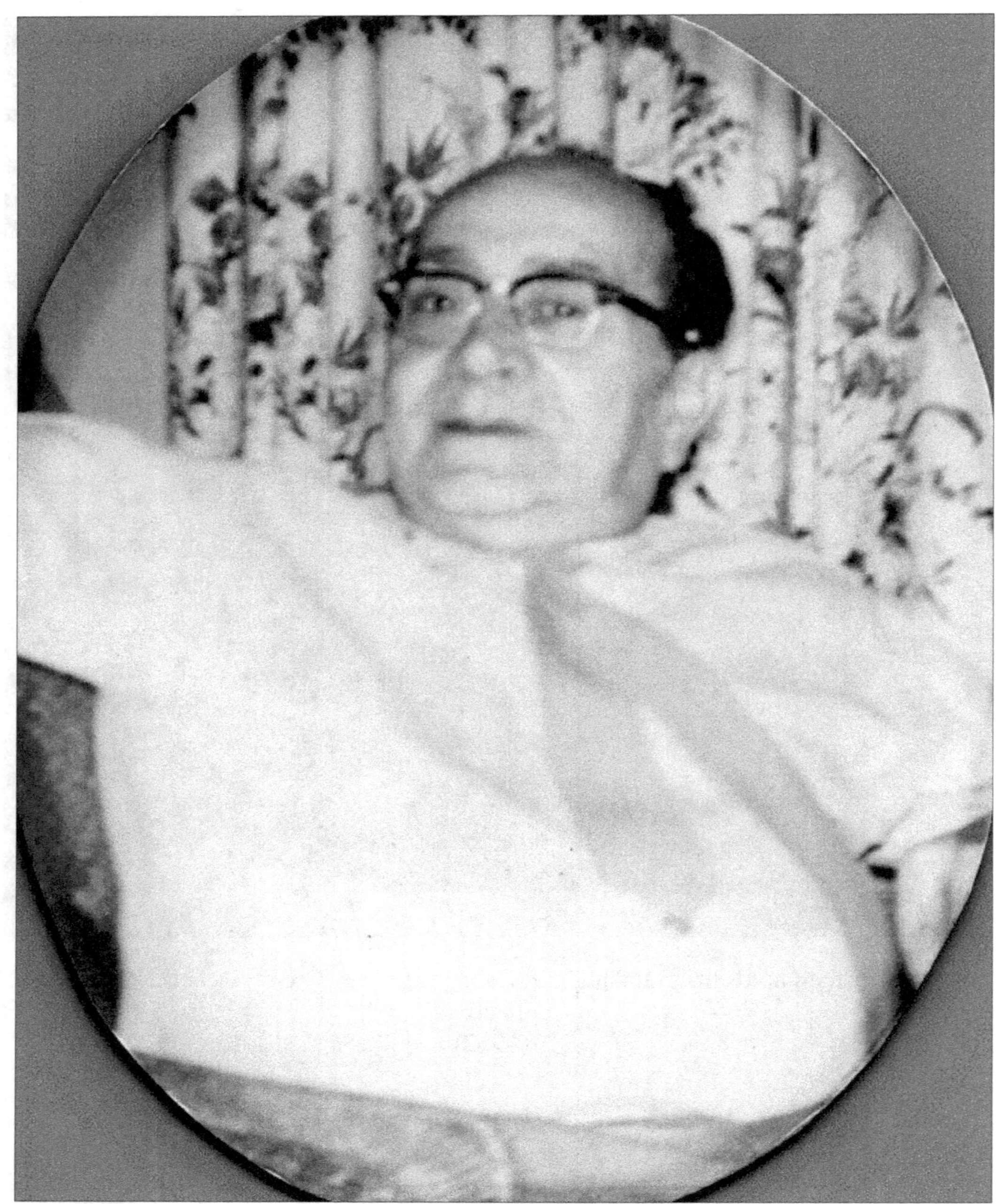

Credit: Rebecca Swanson collection
(about 1959)

Source Citations

1. England & Wales, Christening Index, 1530-1980 (ancestry.com).

2. England, Select Deaths and Burials, 1538-1991 (ancestry.com).

3. 1841 England Census (ancestry.com).

4. 1851 England Census (ancestry.com).

5. England, Sussex, Parish Registers, 1538-1910 (familysearch.org).

6. England, Select Births and Christenings, 1538-1975 (ancestry.com).

7. England & Wales Christening Records, 1530-1906 (ancestry.com).

8. England & Wales, Civil Registration Death Index, 1837-1915 (ancestry.com).

9. 1861 England Census (ancestry.com).

10. England Births and Christenings, 1538-1975 (familysearch.org).

11. England and Wales Death Registration Index 1837-2007 (familysearch.org).

12. England Marriages, 1538–1973 (familysearch.org).

13. 1841 England Census (ancestry.com). .... England & Wales, Christening Index, 1530-1980 (ancestry.com).

14. Ontario, Canada, Deaths, 1869-1936 and Deaths Overseas, 1939-1947 (ancestry.com).

15. England & Wales Marriages, 1538-1940 (ancestry.com).

16. England, Select Marriages, 1538–1973 (ancestry.com).

17. 1851 England Census (ancestry.com). .... England & Wales, Civil Registration Death Index, 1837-1915 (ancestry.com).

18. 1871 England Census (ancestry.com).

19. 1881 England Census (ancestry.com).

20. The Weald of Kent, Surry, and Sussex website (thesurreyweald.org). .... 1891 England Census (ancestry.com).

21. 1901 England Census (familysearch.com).

22. Withyham Parish Registers (theweald.org).

23. 1861 England Census (ancestry.com). .... Withyham Parish Registers (theweald.org).

24. England and Wales Death Registration Index 1837-2007 (familysearch.org). .... 1871 England Census (ancestry.com).

25. 1891 England Census (ancestry.com).

26. 1881 Census of Canada (familysearch.org).

27. 1891 Census of Canada (Ancestry.com).

Source Citations

28. 1901 Census of Canada (ancestry.com).

29. 1911 Census of Canada.

30. Stubbs Family Tree (ancestry.com). .... Ontario, Canada, Deaths, 1869-1938, 1943, and Deaths Overseas, 1939-1947 (ancestry.com).

31. Ontario, Canada, Deaths, 1869-1938, 1943, and Deaths Overseas, 1939-1947 (ancestry.com).

32. Stubbs Family Tree (ancestry.com).

33. U.S., Border Crossings from Canada to U.S., 1895-1956 (ancestry.com).

34. 1921 Census of Canada (ancestry.com).

35. 1891 Census of Canada (Ancestry.com). .... 1871 England Census (ancestry.com).

36. 1887 marriages from MS 932 (http://homepages.rootsweb.ancestry.com/~maryc/1887new.htm).

37. Methodist Church of Canada, *Annual Report of the Missionary Society* (1900).

38. Peter Fancy, *Temiskaming Treasure Trails 1904-1906* (Volume 3 1992).

39. Temiskaming Board of Trade, *Agricultural Temiskaming* (1910).

40. *The Barrie Examiner,* 29 April 1915.

41. *Canadian Grocer,* 7 Apr 1916.

42. Moina W. Large, *History of Ashtabula County, Ohio* (1924).

43. Ontario Marriages, 1869-1927 (familysearch.org).

44. Ontario Deaths, 1869-1937 (familysearch.org).

45. 1911 Census of Canada. .... Ontario Deaths, 1869-1937 (familysearch.org).

46. Ohio Deaths, 1908-1953 (familysearch.org).

47. 1891 Census of Canada (Ancestry.com). .... 1871 England Census (ancestry.com). .... England & Wales, FreeBMD Birth Index (ancestry.com). .... 1900 US Census.

48. Patricia Heasman oral history, 2002.

49. 1910 US Census.

50. Ashtabula County Genealogical Society, *Ashtabula County History, Then and Now* (1985).

51. 1920 US Census. .... 1900 US Census. .... Erie Society for Genealogical Research, *Erie County, Pennsylvania, Naturalizations, 1825-1906* (1983).

52. Pennsylvania, County Marriages, 1885-1950 (familysearch.org).

53. 1900 US Census.

54. U.S. City Directories, 1822-1995 (ancestry.com).

Source Citations

55. 1910 US Census. .... U.S. City Directories, 1822-1995 (ancestry.com).

56. E. D. and W. D Jacobs, *Conneaut City Directory* (1912).

57. *Conneaut News-Herald,* 16 Sep 1919.

58. 1920 US Census.

59. Ohio and Florida, City Directories, 1902-1960 (ancestry.com).

60. 1940 US Census.

61. Ashtabula County Genealogical Society, *Ashtabula County History, Then and Now* (1985), article by Laura J. Heasman.

62. Gleenwood Cemetery (Conneaut) Transcriptions (www.conneautohio.us). .... 1881 Census of Canada (familysearch.org). .... Ohio Deaths, 1908-1953 (familysearch.org). .... Ontario Births, 1869-1912 (familysearch.org).

63. Gleenwood Cemetery (Conneaut) Transcriptions (www.conneautohio.us). .... Ohio Deaths, 1908-1953 (familysearch.org).

64. Moina W. Large, *History of Ashtabula County, Ohio* (1924). .... *Conneaut News-Herald,* 16 Sep 1919. .... Ohio, County Marriages, 1789-2013 (familysearch.org).

65. Ohio, County Marriages, 1789-2013 (familysearch.org).

66. 1900 US Census. .... Gleenwood Cemetery (Conneaut) Transcriptions (www.conneautohio.us). .... Social Security Death Index (ancestry.com). .... Pennsylvania Births and Christenings, 1709-1950 (familysearch.com).

67. Gleenwood Cemetery (Conneaut) Transcriptions (www.conneautohio.us). .... Social Security Death Index (ancestry.com).

68. Patricia Heasman oral history.

69. *Conneaut News-Herald,* 14 Jun 1972.

70. Find-A-Grave (www.findagrave.com).

71. Ontario Marriages, 1869-1927 (familysearch.org). .... British Columbia Death Registrations, 1872-1986; 1992-1993 (familysearch.org).

72. British Columbia Death Registrations, 1872-1986; 1992-1993 (familysearch.org).

73. 1906 Canada Census of Manitoba, Saskatchewan, and Alberta (familysearch.org).

74. Canada, Voters Lists, 1935-1980 (familysearch.org).

75. Ontario Births, 1869-1911 (familysearch.org).

76. Ontario Marriages, 1869-1927 (familysearch.org). .... 1911 Census of Canada.

77. California Death Index, 1905-1939 (familysearch.org).

78. California Death Records 1940-1997 (familysearch.org). .... Indiana, Death Certificates, 1899-2011 (ancestry.com).

79. California Death Records 1940-1997 (familysearch.org).

80. 1901 Census of Canada (ancestry.com). .... Ontario Births, 1869-1911 (familysearch.org).

81. Soldiers of the First World War: 1914-1918 (http://www.bac-lac.gc.ca/).

82. East Grinstead Parish Registers (theweald.org).

83. England & Wales Christening Records, 1530-1906 (ancestry.com). .... England Marriages, 1538–1973 (familysearch.org). .... Stubbs Family Tree (ancestry.com).

84. England & Wales, FreeBMD Death Index: 1837-1915 (ancestry.com). .... Stubbs Family Tree (ancestry.com).

85. England Marriages, 1538–1973 (familysearch.org). .... Stubbs Family Tree (ancestry.com). .... 1841 England Census (ancestry.com). .... 1851 England Census (ancestry.com).

86. England & Wales Marriages, 1538-1940 (ancestry.com). .... Stubbs Family Tree (ancestry.com). .... England and Wales Death Registration Index 1837-2007 (familysearch.org).

87. Stubbs Family Tree (ancestry.com). .... England & Wales, Civil Registration Death Index, 1837-1915 (ancestry.com).

88. 1851 England Census (ancestry.com). .... Stubbs Family Tree (ancestry.com).

89. Stubbs Family Tree (ancestry.com). .... England & Wales Marriages, 1538-1940 (ancestry.com).

90. 1911 England Census (ancestry.com).

91. 1803-1814 Upper Inismacsaint Parish Baptism Extracts FHC # 0992663 (www.rootsweb.ancestry.com).

92. 1862 Householders vicinity of Derrygonnelly (census) (www.rootsweb.ancestry.com). .... Griffith's Valuation of 1862.

93. Ireland, Select Marriages, 1619-1898 (ancestry.com).

94. Ontario, Canada, County Marriage Registers, 1858-1869 (ancestry.com).

95. Ontario, Canada, Deaths, 1869-1936 and Deaths Overseas, 1939-1947 (ancestry.com). .... 1901 Census of Canada (ancestry.com).

96. Marriage record Benmore Church of Ireland. .... Ireland Marriages, 1619-1898 (familysearch.org).

97. Ontario, Canada Marriages, 1801-1926 (ancestry.com). .... Ontario, Canada, Marriages, 1801-1928, 1933-1934 (ancestry.com).

98. Ontario, Canada, County Marriage Registers, 1858-1869 (ancestry.com). .... 1901 Census of Canada (ancestry.com).

99. 1901 Census of Canada (ancestry.com). .... Find-A-Grave (www.findagrave.com). .... 1881 Census of Canada (familysearch.org).

100. Find-A-Grave (www.findagrave.com). .... Ontario, Canada, Deaths, 1869-1938, 1943-1944, and Deaths Overseas, 1939-1947 (ancestry.com).

101. 1901 Census of Canada (ancestry.com). .... Topic: Allingham and Magan marriage 1854

Source Citations

(http://www.rootschat.com).

102. 1871 Census of Canada. .... 1881 Census of Canada (familysearch.org). .... Ontario, Canada, Deaths, 1869-1938, 1943-1944, and Deaths Overseas, 1939-1947 (ancestry.com).

103. Marriage record Benmore Church of Ireland.

104. 1871 Census of Canada.

105. 1881 Census of Canada (familysearch.org). .... Pennsylvania, Find A Grave Index, 1681-2011 (ancestry.com).

106. Find-A-Grave (www.findagrave.com). .... Pennsylvania, Find A Grave Index, 1681-2011 (ancestry.com).

107. 1930 US Census.

108. Pennsylvania, Death Certificates, 1906-1964 (ancestry.com).

109. Erie, Pennsylvania City Directories, 1889-93 (ancestry.com).

110. 1881 Census of Canada (familysearch.org). .... 1871 Census of Canada.

111. Ontario, Canada, Marriages, 1801-1928, 1933-1934 (ancestry.com).

112. 1881 Census of Canada (familysearch.org). .... Ontario, Canada, Deaths, 1869-1936 and Deaths Overseas, 1939-1947 (ancestry.com).

113. 1901 Census of Canada (ancestry.com). .... Ontario, Canada, Marriages, 1801-1928, 1933-1934 (ancestry.com).

114. Ontario, Canada, Marriages, 1801-1928, 1933-1934 (ancestry.com). .... 1891 Census of Canada (Ancestry.com).

115. Fermanagh Griffiths Valuation.

116. World War I Draft Registration Cards, 1917-1918 (ancestry.com).

117. Greenwood Cemetery LaPorte (http://www.dunelady.com/laporte/cemeteries/greenwood). .... Ohio Deaths, 1908-1932, 1938-1944, and 1958-2007 (ancestry.com).

118. 1930 US Census. .... Ohio, County Marriages, 1789-2013 (familysearch.org).

119. England, Select Deaths and Burials, 1538-1991 (ancestry.com). .... England, Sussex, Parish Registers, 1538-1910 (familysearch.org).

120. East Grinstead Marriage Registers (http://thesurreyweald.org/).

121. West Hoathly Parish Registers (theweald.org).

122. Maresfield Parish Registers (theweald.org).

123. England Marriages, 1538–1973 (familysearch.org). .... England, Sussex, Parish Registers, 1538-1910 (familysearch.org).

124. Beryl Offley's records (theweald.org).

Source Citations

125. England Deaths and Burials, 1538-1991 (familysearch.org).

126. Clandestine Marriages and Baptisms in Fleet Prison, King's Bench Prison, the Mint and the May Fair Chapel, 1667-c1777 (bmdregisters.co.uk).

127. Tree: Frater Family (http://rjfrater.com). .... England & Wales Christening Records, 1530-1906 (ancestry.com).

128. Tree: Frater Family (http://rjfrater.com).

129. Frater Family by Christine (ancestry.com). .... England & Wales Marriages, 1538-1940 (ancestry.com).

130. England, Select Deaths and Burials, 1538-1991 (ancestry.com). .... England & Wales, Civil Registration Death Index, 1837-1915 (ancestry.com).

131. England & Wales Christening Records, 1530-1906 (ancestry.com). .... England & Wales Marriages, 1538-1940 (ancestry.com).

132. England & Wales, FreeBMD Death Index: 1837-1915 (ancestry.com).

133. Harvey History 071117 website (http://harveyhistory.info). .... England Births and Christenings, 1538-1975 (familysearch.org).

134. Steep Parish Records (findmypast.co.uk). .... Steep church registers (Steep History Group).

135. Hampshire, England, Extracted Parish Records (ancestry.com).

136. Steep Parish Records (findmypast.co.uk).

137. Steep church registers (Steep History Group).

138. England, Select Births and Christenings, 1538-1975 (ancestry.com). .... East Meon parish registers (eastmeonhistory.org.uk).

139. Hampshire baptisms (findmypast.com).

140. England, Select Births and Christenings, 1538-1975 (ancestry.com). .... Steep church registers (Steep History Group). .... 1851 England Census (ancestry.com).

141. England & Wales, Civil Registration Death Index, 1837-1915 (ancestry.com). .... England, Select Deaths and Burials, 1538-1991 (ancestry.com).

142. Annette Platt, "Heasman: Horstead Parva & East Grinstead" (email 11 April 2009). .... R.P. Crawfurd, *East Grinstead Parish Register, 1558-1661* (Sussex Record Society, 1917, retrieved from http://www05.us.archive.org). .... England, Select Births and Christenings, 1538-1975 (ancestry.com). .... Sussex Record Society, *Sussex Record Society,* Volume 24.

143. England, Select Deaths and Burials, 1538-1991 (ancestry.com). .... England Deaths and Burials, 1538-1991 (familysearch.org).

144. R.P. Crawfurd, *East Grinstead Parish Register, 1558-1661* (Sussex Record Society, 1917, retrieved from http://www05.us.archive.org).

145. D.J.H. Clifford, *St. Margaret's Church West Hoathly Burials 1606 -1900* (westhoathly.org.uk).

146. Sussex Marriage Registers (theweald.org). .... Edwin H.W. Dunkin, *Calendar of Sussex Marriage*

Source Citations

Licences Recorded in the Consistory Court of the Bishop of Chichester for the Archdeaconry of Lewes (1901).

147. Annette Platt, "Heasman: Horstead Parva & East Grinstead" (email 11 April 2009). .... Edwin H.W. Dunkin, *Calendar of Sussex Marriage Licences Recorded in the Consistory Court of the Bishop of Chichester for the Archdeaconry of Lewes* (1901).

148. Annette Platt, "Heasman: Horstead Parva & East Grinstead" (email 11 April 2009). .... D.J.H. Clifford, *St. Margaret's Church West Hoathly Burials 1606 -1900* (westhoathly.org.uk).

149. R.P. Crawfurd, *East Grinstead Parish Register, 1558-1661* (Sussex Record Society, 1917, retrieved from http://www05.us.archive.org). .... England Births and Christenings, 1538-1975 (familysearch.org).

150. England & Wales, Prerogative Court of Canterbury Wills, 1384-1858 (ancestry.com), Will of Sarah Medhurst 1702.

151. England & Wales, Christening Index, 1530-1980 (ancestry.com). .... Will of George Cornwell, of Framfield (13 Oct 1694). .... Will of John Cornwell of Framfield (3 Aug 1715).

152. Derek Miller, *The Lineage and History of the Muddle Families of the World, including variants Muddel, Muddell, Mudle and Moddle* (2011). .... England, Select Deaths and Burials, 1538-1991 (ancestry.com).

153. Mitchell and Hughes, *The Marriage Registers of the Parish Church of All Saints, Maidstone* (1901). .... England, Select Marriages, 1538–1973 (ancestry.com).

154. Will of George Cornwell, of Framfield (13 Oct 1694).

155. The Weald of Kent, Surry, and Sussex website (thesurreyweald.org).

156. Ringmer Parish Registers (theweald.org).

157. Framfield Marriage Registers (theweald.org).

158. *Abstracts of probate acts in the Prerogative Court of Canterbury* (1902-1926).

159. Will of Elizabeth Browne 7 Jan 1684.

160. Withyham Burial Registers (theweald.org).

161. *Sussex Record Society* (Volume 1 1902).

162. East Sussex Record Office, SAS-WH/328.

163. Gravestone picture (gravestonephotos.com).

164. East Meon parish registers (eastmeonhistory.org.uk).

165. F. W. T Attree, *Post Mortem Inquistions 1485 - 1649* (1912).

166. 2007 Survey of Barcombe and Hamsey ("Complete Tenements") (bandhpast.co.uk). .... East Sussex Record Office, Will: William Heasman of Little Horsted, yeoman - 1615.

167. Buxted Marriage Registers (theweald.org).

168. East Sussex Record Office, Will: William Heasman of Barcombe - 1559.

169. F. W. T Attree, *Post Mortem Inquistions 1485 - 1649* (1912). .... East Sussex Record Office, Will: John

Heasman of Barcombe, husbandman - 1558.

170. East Sussex Record Office, Will: John Heasman of Barcombe, husbandman - 1558.

171. East Sussex Record Office, Will of Ralph Groombridge of Withyham.

172. Will of Ralph Groombridge 1646.

173. England Births and Christenings, 1538-1975 (familysearch.org). .... England Marriages, 1538–1973 (familysearch.org).

174. Ashtabula County Genealogical Society, *Ashtabula County History, Then and Now* (1985). .... Conversations with Patricia Ann Eagles.

175. *Conneaut News-Herald,* 11 Oct 1919.

176. 1930 US Census. .... Ohio and Florida, City Directories, 1902-1960 (ancestry.com).

177. *Conneaut News-Herald,* abt 1960.

178. U.S. Army, Register of Enlistments, 1798-1914 (ancestry.com).

179. Conversations with Patricia Ann Eagles.

180. *The Ashtabula Star Beacon.*

181. 1930 US Census. .... Gleenwood Cemetery (Conneaut) Transcriptions (www.conneautohio.us). .... Ohio Deaths, 1908-1932, 1938-1944, and 1958-2007 (ancestry.com).

182. Gleenwood Cemetery (Conneaut) Transcriptions (www.conneautohio.us).

183. Nonconformist Register, Sussex (thesurreyweald.org). .... England & Wales, Christening Index, 1530-1980 (ancestry.com). .... England & Wales, Non-Conformist and Non-Parochial Registers, 1567-1970 (ancestry.com). .... England Births and Christenings, 1538-1975 (familysearch.org).

184. England and Wales Non-Conformist Record Indexes (RG4-8), 1588-1977 (familysearch.org).

185. Nonconformist Register, Sussex (thesurreyweald.org). .... England & Wales, Non-Conformist and Non-Parochial Registers, 1567-1970 (ancestry.com).

186. Nonconformist Register, Sussex (thesurreyweald.org).

187. Hartfield Parish Registers (theweald.org).

188. Public Record Office of Northern Ireland, *Freeholders' records* (http://www.proni.gov.uk).

189. National Archives of Ireland, Ireland Valuation Office Books (findmypast.co.uk).

190. The Weald of Kent, Surry, and Sussex website (thesurreyweald.org). .... East Grinstead Parish Registers (theweald.org).

191. Will of John Turk proven 4th August 1847. .... England & Wales, Civil Registration Death Index, 1837-1915 (ancestry.com).

192. Hampshire, England, Extracted Parish Records (ancestry.com). .... William John Charles Moens, *Hampshire Allegations for Marriage Licences Granted by the Bishop of Winchester, 1689 to 1837, Volume 2*

Source Citations

(1893).

193. Hampshire, England, Extracted Parish Records (ancestry.com). .... William John Charles Moens, *Hampshire Allegations for Marriage Licences Granted by the Bishop of Winchester, 1689 to 1837, Volume 2* (1893). .... East Meon parish registers (eastmeonhistory.org.uk).

194. Harvey History 071117 website (http://harveyhistory.info). .... East Meon Parish Records (findmypast.com).

195. East Meon Parish Records (findmypast.com).

196. Harvey History 071117 website (http://harveyhistory.info).

197. Ropley, Hampshire Parish Records (findmypast.co.uk).

198. Harvey History 071117 website (http://harveyhistory.info). .... Ropley, Hampshire Parish Records (findmypast.co.uk). .... Gravestone in Ropley, Hampshire.

199. Harvey History 071117 website (http://harveyhistory.info). .... England & Wales, National Probate Calendar (Index of Wills and Administrations), 1858-1966, 1973-1995 (ancestry.com).

200. Harvey History 071117 website (http://harveyhistory.info). .... England, Select Deaths and Burials, 1538-1991 (ancestry.com). .... Gravestone in Ropley, Hampshire.

201. England & Wales Christening Records, 1530-1906 (ancestry.com). .... Harvey History 071117 website (http://harveyhistory.info).

202. England & Wales, National Probate Calendar (Index of Wills and Administrations), 1858-1966, 1973-1995 (ancestry.com).

203. Email from Judy Stubbs.

204. England, Sussex, Parish Registers, 1538-1910 (familysearch.org). .... England, Select Births and Christenings, 1538-1975 (ancestry.com).

205. 1851 England Census (ancestry.com). .... Steep church registers (Steep History Group).

206. UK, Poll Books and Electoral Registers, 1538-1893 (ancestry.com).

207. Gravestone picture (gravestonephotos.com). .... England, Select Births and Christenings, 1538-1975 (ancestry.com).

208. Gravestone picture (gravestonephotos.com). .... England, Select Deaths and Burials, 1538-1991 (ancestry.com).

209. Diane Lyng's records on The Weald (http://theweald.org).

210. R.P. Crawfurd, *East Grinstead Parish Register, 1558-1661* (Sussex Record Society, 1917, retrieved from http://www05.us.archive.org). .... Diane Lyng's records on The Weald (http://theweald.org).

211. R.P. Crawfurd, *East Grinstead Parish Register, 1558-1661* (Sussex Record Society, 1917, retrieved from http://www05.us.archive.org). .... Sussex Record Society, *Sussex Record Society,* Volume 24.

212. Diane Lyng's records on The Weald (http://theweald.org). .... England, Select Births and Christenings, 1538-1975 (ancestry.com).

Source Citations

213. *Court Book of the Manor of Rotherfield, 1631 - 1724* (discovery.nationalarchives.gov.uk).

214. England, Select Deaths and Burials, 1538-1991 (ancestry.com). .... *Will of Thomas Browne 30 Aug 1734*.

215. Gravestone picture (gravestonephotos.com). .... England Deaths and Burials, 1538-1991 (familysearch.org).

216. H. A. L. Fisher, *James Bryce V2: Viscount Bryce of Dechmon* (1927).

217. Edwin H.W. Dunkin, *Calendar of Sussex Marriage Licences Recorded in the Consistory Court of the Bishop of Chichester for the Archdeaconry of Lewes* (1901).

218. Sussex Archaeological Society, *Sussex archaeological collections relating to the history and antiquities of the county*.

219. 2007 Survey of Barcombe and Hamsey ("Complete Tenements") (bandhpast.co.uk).

220. Sussex Archaeological Society, *Sussex archaeological collections relating to the history and antiquities of the county*. .... William Smith Ellis, *The Parks and Forests of Sussex* (1885).

221. Sussex Archaeological Society, *Sussex archaeological collections relating to the history and antiquities of the county,* Vol 22.

222. Sussex Archaeological Society, *Sussex archaeological collections relating to the history and antiquities of the county,* Vol 23.

223. Annette Platt, "Heasman: Horstead Parva & East Grinstead" (email 11 April 2009). .... Diane Lyng's records on The Weald (http://theweald.org). .... England, Select Births and Christenings, 1538-1975 (ancestry.com).

224. R.P. Crawfurd, *East Grinstead Parish Register, 1558-1661* (Sussex Record Society, 1917, retrieved from http://www05.us.archive.org). .... England, Select Births and Christenings, 1538-1975 (ancestry.com).

225. Mitchell and Hughes, *The Marriage Registers of the Parish Church of All Saints, Maidstone* (1901).

226. England, Select Births and Christenings, 1538-1975 (ancestry.com). .... Will of George Cornwell, of Framfield (13 Oct 1694).

227. Will of John Cornwell of Framfield (3 Aug 1715).

228. Will of George Cornwell, of Framfield (13 Oct 1694). .... Will of John Cornwell of Framfield (3 Aug 1715).

229. Frederick William Jewitt Llewellyn, *The Reliquary and illustrated archaeologist,: a quarterly journal and review* (1902).

230. Sussex Record Society, *Sussex Record Society* (Volume 6).

231. Will of William Browne 1674.

232. East Sussex Record Office, Will: William Heasman of Little Horsted, yeoman - 1615.

233. *Sussex Record Society* (Volume 1 1902). .... Church of England Diocese of Chichester, *Calendar of Sussex Marriage Licenses: Recorded in the Consistory Court of the Bishop of Chichester for the Archdeaconry of Lewes* (1902).

234. East Sussex Record Office, Will: Jone Hessman of Little Horsted, widow - 1568.

Name Index

Name Index

Name Index

Name Index

Name Index

Name Index

HEASMAN

Name Index

Name Index

Name Index

Name Index

Name Index

Name Index

Name Index

Name Index